INTRODUCING
ISSUES WITH
OPPOSING
VIEWPOINTS®

Alternative Medicine

Jacqueline Langwith, *Book Editor*

GREENHAVEN PRESS
A part of Gale, Cengage Learning

GALE
CENGAGE Learning™

Detroit • New York • San Francisco • New Haven, Conn • Waterville, Maine • London

Christine Nasso, *Publisher*
Elizabeth Des Chenes, *Managing Editor*

LIBRARY OF CONGRESS CATALOGING-IN-PUBLICATION DATA

Alternative medicine / Jacqueline Langwith, book editor.
    p. cm. — (Introducing issues with opposing viewpoints)
Includes bibliographical references and index.
ISBN 978-0-7377-4333-3 (hardcover)
1. Alternative medicine—Juvenile literature. I. Langwith, Jacqueline.
R733.A4586 2009
610—dc22

2008053349

Printed in the United States of America
1 2 3 4 5 6 7 13 12 11 10 09

Contents

Chapter 3: What Role Should Alternative Medicine Play in Health Care in the United States?

Foreword

Indulging in a wide spectrum of ideas, beliefs, and perspectives is a critical cornerstone of democracy. After all, it is often debates over differences of opinion, such as whether to legalize abortion, how to treat prisoners, or when to enact the death penalty, that shape our society and drive it forward. Such diversity of thought is frequently regarded as the hallmark of a healthy and civilized culture. As the Reverend Clifford Schutjer of the First Congregational Church in Mansfield, Ohio, declared in a 2001 sermon, "Surrounding oneself with only like-minded people, restricting what we listen to or read only to what we find agreeable is irresponsible. Refusing to entertain doubts once we make up our minds is a subtle but deadly form of arrogance." With this advice in mind, Introducing Issues with Opposing Viewpoints books aim to open readers' minds to the critically divergent views that comprise our world's most important debates.

Introducing Issues with Opposing Viewpoints simplifies for students the enormous and often overwhelming mass of material now available via print and electronic media. Collected in every volume is an array of opinions that captures the essence of a particular controversy or topic. Introducing Issues with Opposing Viewpoints books embody the spirit of nineteenth-century journalist Charles A. Dana's axiom: "Fight for your opinions, but do not believe that they contain the whole truth, or the only truth." Absorbing such contrasting opinions teaches students to analyze the strength of an argument and compare it to its opposition. From this process readers can inform and strengthen their own opinions, or be exposed to new information that will change their minds. Introducing Issues with Opposing Viewpoints is a mosaic of different voices. The authors are statesmen, pundits, academics, journalists, corporations, and ordinary people who have felt compelled to share their experiences and ideas in a public forum. Their words have been collected from newspapers, journals, books, speeches, interviews, and the Internet, the fastest growing body of opinionated material in the world.

Introducing Issues with Opposing Viewpoints shares many of the well-known features of its critically acclaimed parent series, Opposing Viewpoints. The articles are presented in a pro/con format, allowing readers to absorb divergent perspectives side by side. Active reading questions preface each viewpoint, requiring the student to approach the material thoughtfully and carefully. Useful charts, graphs, and cartoons supplement each article. A thorough introduction provides readers with crucial background on an issue. An annotated bibliography points the reader toward articles, books, and Web sites that contain additional information on the topic. An appendix of organizations to contact contains a wide variety of charities, nonprofit organizations, political groups, and private enterprises that each hold a position on the issue at hand. Finally, a comprehensive index allows readers to locate content quickly and efficiently.

Introducing Issues with Opposing Viewpoints is also significantly different from Opposing Viewpoints. As the series title implies, its presentation will help introduce students to the concept of opposing viewpoints and learn to use this material to aid in critical writing and debate. The series' four-color, accessible format makes the books attractive and inviting to readers of all levels. In addition, each viewpoint has been carefully edited to maximize a reader's understanding of the content. Short but thorough viewpoints capture the essence of an argument. A substantial, thought-provoking essay question placed at the end of each viewpoint asks the student to further investigate the issues raised in the viewpoint, compare and contrast two authors' arguments, or consider how one might go about forming an opinion on the topic at hand. Each viewpoint contains sidebars that include at-a-glance information and handy statistics. A Facts About section located in the back of the book further supplies students with relevant facts and figures.

Following in the tradition of the Opposing Viewpoints series, Greenhaven Press continues to provide readers with invaluable exposure to the controversial issues that shape our world. As John Stuart Mill once wrote: "The only way in which a human being can make some approach to knowing the whole of a subject is by hearing what can be said about it by persons of every variety of opinion and studying all modes in which it can be looked at by every character of mind. No wise man ever acquired his wisdom in any mode but this." It is to this principle that Introducing Issues with Opposing Viewpoints books are dedicated.

Introduction

"No amount of Prozac can do what music can do."

—Composer and musician David Amram

"They [alternative medicine proponents] include such things as music therapy, as though anything that makes us feel better is now medicine."

—Physics professor Bob Park

Music is a fundamental part of human life in the twenty-first century. Americans take music with them wherever they go using iPods and MP3 players. U.S. soldiers in Iraq use rap music to gear up for battle and express feelings of fear. Athletes use music to calm their nerves and prepare for a race. Teenagers use music as a form of expression as they transition into adulthood. Musical performances in parks, at nightclubs, or at large concert halls provide a means of socializing. For thousands of years, music has been associated with important cultural ceremonies, such as weddings, funerals, graduations, and presidential inaugurations. Music means so many things to humanity, and it is not surprising that it is also used as a form of healing art. Many people believe music can be used to heal people suffering from mental and physical diseases. However, other people think that while music may help people feel good, there is no evidence to show that it heals people.

Music and medicine have been intertwined since ancient times. In ancient Greece Apollo was considered both the god of music and the god of medicine. Apollo is most often pictured holding a lyre, and it was said that he was a gifted musician. Apollo was seen as a god who had the ability not only to cure, but also to bring ill health. In ancient China healing was considered music's primary purpose. In fact, the Chinese character *yao*, which means medicine, is derived from the character *yue*, which means music. A form of ancient Chinese music called "elegant music" was believed to have a beneficial effect on the human body.

In modern America the recognition that music could help alleviate the pain and trauma suffered by soldiers led to the establishment of the profession of music therapy. According to the American Music Therapy Association (AMTA), after World War I and during World War II, it became common for local musicians to play for wounded soldiers at veterans' hospitals around the country. Soldiers suffering both physical and mental trauma responded so favorably to the music that after World War II, doctors and nurses began requesting that the hospitals hire musicians. It soon became evident that these hospital musicians needed some prior training before interacting with patients, and the demand started growing for trained music therapists. The first music therapy degree program in the world was founded at Michigan State University in 1944. Today there are at least seventy-five colleges offering degrees in music therapy.

Author and pediatric psychiatrist O.J. Sahler explains what music therapy involves and how it can be used to help people suffering from medical diseases and disorders:

> There are many different facets of music therapy. It can involve listening to live or recorded music. It can also be about making music. You can make music by playing a particular piece that you know or learn, or you can write your own music. The music therapist can also write music to go with words that patients have written. And sometimes the music therapist will ask people what their favorite songs are and do what we call lyric analysis. That will explore why a particular song resonates with the patient.

According to the AMTA, music therapy can help children and adolescents suffering from developmental and learning disabilities, elderly patients suffering from Alzheimer's disease, mothers in labor, and people of any age suffering from mental illness, substance abuse problems, brain injuries, physical disabilities, and acute or chronic pain.

Many people believe in the power of music therapy. In a 2008 radio interview broadcast on WNYC in New York City, Clive Robbins, cofounder of the Nordoff-Robbins Center for Music Therapy in the United Kingdom, described a music therapy session involving Anna, a treatment-resistant, eleven-year-old, blind, wheelchair-bound young girl suffering from cerebral palsy. The music therapist was Robbins's partner, Paul Nordoff. Anna was generally sullen and would not engage or communicate with anyone. However, when she entered the room where the session was taking place, she uttered, "I at school." Nordoff then began playing music and singing "I at school," and the two began singing back and forth to each other. The tone, tempo, and pitch of Nordoff's singing and each chord he played on the piano were designed to elicit a particular response. Anna responded in sync, matching his tempo and tone or stepping it up or down. She was totally present, engaged, and excited. Robbins says, "Music can bypass areas of disability because of what music is—the healthy part of us all."

Author and neurologist Oliver Sacks believes music is therapeutic. In his memoir, *Awakenings,* which was turned into a movie starring actors Robert De Niro and Robin Williams, Sacks wrote about how music awoke victims of encephalitis lethargica, a mysterious disease causing people to become catatonic. Sacks writes:

> Their voices, if they could speak, lacked tone and force: they were almost spectral. Yet these patients were able to sing, loudly and clearly, with a normal range of expressiveness and tone. Among those who could walk and talk, although only in a jerky, broken way, music gave their movement or speech the steadiness and control it usually lacked. We could observe this effect on the patients' electroencephalograms [EEGs]. If we found music that worked, their EEGs, often exceedingly slow, reflecting their frozen states, would become faster and more regular. We noted this when patients listened to music or sang it or played it, even when they imagined it.

In the twenty-first century, scientists are using advanced imaging techniques like magnetic resonance imaging (MRI) and positron emission tomography (PET) to try to understand what happens in the brain when patients participate in music therapy sessions. Brain imaging has revealed how music therapy may be helping improve the speech of some stroke victims who have damage to the left sides of their brains. These patients generally cannot talk, since the left part of the brain is the center of speech. Music therapy appears to increase the ability of the right side of the brain to take over some of the functions for the left brain. According to Oliver Sacks, music therapy is a "tool of great power in many neurological disorders because of its unique capacity to organize or reorganize cerebral function when it has been damaged."

Many doctors are skeptical of claims that music has actual therapeutic effects. Steven Novella, a clinical neurologist and the president and cofounder of the New England Skeptical Society, is one of these doctors. According to Novella, "music is very powerful for humans," but there is no scientific evidence to suggest that music is doing anything special to "heal" the brain. Novella uses an analogy to make his point. He says playing soccer provides many benefits for children. It helps fights obesity and helps develop teamwork and other social skills. However, says Novella, we do not call soccer "soccer therapy." He believes music is a "fine tool" that can be used to help patients relax, communicate better, or feel better. However, he is uncomfortable with the term "music therapy" because he says that music itself does not heal the brain.

No one disputes that music is, and always has been, a powerful medium. However, while some people, such as Oliver Sacks, believe that music is powerful enough to heal the brain, others, such as Steven Novella, think it just makes us feel good. Debates similar to this one surround alternative medicines. Some people believe practices such as acupuncture, chiropractic, and homeopathy are powerful healing mediums, but others believe they only make us think we are feeling better. In *Introducing Issues with Opposing Viewpoints: Alternative Medicine*, the contributing authors discuss the merits of alternative medicine in the following chapters: "Is Alternative Medicine Effective?" "Does Alternative Medicine Help Fight Disease?" and "What Role Should Alternative Medicine Play in Health Care in the United States?"

Chapter 1

Is Alternative Medicine Effective?

A family reviews X-rays with a chiropractor. Chiropractic is just one of the many forms of alternative medicine.

Acupuncture Is Effective

Mike Adams

"If they can keep acupuncture trapped in a small box of so-called 'approved uses,' they can effectively marginalize this entire field. . . . But the reality is that acupuncture has far greater potential than this."

In the following viewpoint Mike Adams contends that modern medicine is blind to the real benefits of acupuncture. Adams believes that most Western medical doctors regard acupuncture as a false science and fail to see that this ancient practice can do more than cure nausea or ease pain. According to Adams, acupuncture can treat many ailments, even taking the place of surgery and prescription medications. Adams believes that someday a revolution will take place, and modern medicine will finally accept acupuncture and its full healing potential. Adams is an author, consumer advocate, and the editor of *NaturalNews.com*.

AS YOU READ, CONSIDER THE FOLLOWING QUESTIONS:

1. Name one of the things that Adams says is interesting about the study conducted in Sydney, Australia.
2. According to Adams, in acupuncture there is a relationship between the practitioner and the patient on what kind of level?
3. What does Adams refer to as the "profit centers" for Western medicine?

Mike Adams, "Acupuncture Proven Effective at Treating Post-Operative Nausea; but Modern Medicine Marginalizes True Potential of Acupuncture," *Natural News,* August 3, 2004. © 2004 The Natural News Network. All rights reserved. Reproduced by permission.

A cupuncture has proven itself useful yet again in a study conducted in Sydney, Australia that focused on the use of a single acupuncture point, the P6 point, as a point for treating post-operative nausea. The study showed that those who received the acupuncture treatment on their P6 point were 28% less likely to feel nauseous, and 29% less likely to be sick than patients who did not receive the treatment, or who received sham treatments, such as insertion of the needle at the wrong point.

There are a couple of interesting points to note about this study. First, this is yet more evidence that acupuncture is in fact quite useful, not only in treating nausea, but in altering the nature of the mind-body connection in patients. But the really interesting thing about this study is only obvious when you zoom out and look at the big picture here. This was conducted by the insertion of a single needle at a single point. That's not something that an experienced acupuncture practitioner would typically do. Acupuncture is not so rigid as to be limited to a single insertion at a single point.

Science and Art

When acupuncture is pursued in the traditional way, it is as much a form of art as it is science. An experienced acupuncture practitioner will insert many needles at many points, and will not be controlled by a rigid set of guidelines prescribing a certain set of points. Acupuncture doesn't work in that way. You can't say just because a patient has symptoms A, B, and C, therefore you should insert needles at points P5, P6, and so on.

Acupuncture is more intimate than that. There is a relationship between the practitioner and the patient on an energetic level. The practitioner observes and senses the condition of the patient and how they react to the insertion of the first few needles, and then the practitioner modifies their plan accordingly. They may insert as many as 30 needles at different points, and those points would vary from one patient to the next, even if they showed the exact same symptoms. That's because each patient is unique. Each patient has a different energy system, a different physical makeup, a different posture, a different pattern of energy expression, and so on. There are so many factors involved that it would be impossible to try to quantify them in a rigid, scientific way.

Acupuncture is more than just taking a needle and inserting it at a certain point, and yet, even doing so appears to work quite well in rigid scientific studies. Imagine how much stronger the effect of acupuncture would be if the studies allowed experienced acupuncture practitioners to pursue their art form to its fullest.

Marginalized by Modern Medicine

There's another thing that's worth noting here: until recently, modern medicine was very uncomfortable with the idea of integrating acupuncture at all. In fact, there are still many old school doctors and so-called anti-quackery doctors who still rail against acupuncture, completely unaware of all the scientific evidence proving its efficacy. The Western system of medicine simply isn't comfortable with the idea that physicians from 5,000 years ago in ancient China knew more about health than doctors do today, and yet this is most certainly the case. Acupuncture is a traditional treatment dating back many thousands of years in China, and if you read the ancient Chinese texts on this subject, as I have, you will find that the doctors of that time in China knew far more about the nature of the human spirit and the human body and how health really operates than most Western doctors do today. In fact, it's almost laughable to try to compare the knowledge of body wisdom in today's doctors versus the wisdom of people from 5,000 years ago.

So, for many decades, modern medicine fought the idea that acupuncture could work at all, and once again, there's still a lot of denial (especially in the minds of older doctors) that acupuncture has any use whatsoever. For the more pioneering doctors in modern organized medicine, they are beginning to accept acupuncture, but only as a complementary therapy.

Notice that in this study, a surgical procedure was performed on patients, and then acupuncture was only allowed to be used to treat

FAST FACT

According to the 2002 National Health Interview Survey, 8.2 million U.S. adults reported making use of acupuncture at one time in their lives, and 2.13 million reported recent use of the ancient medicine.

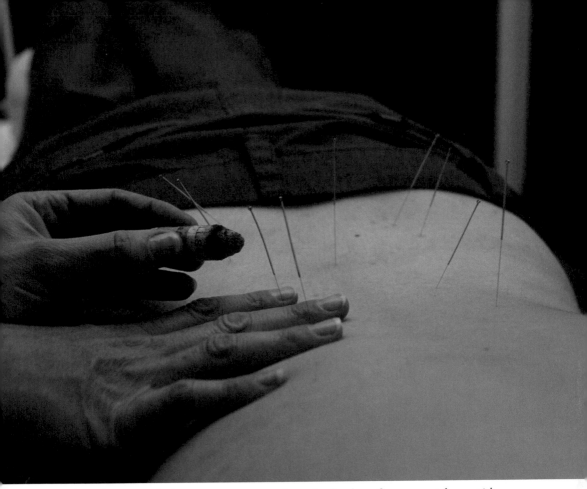

The author contends that acupuncture can often take the place of surgery, catalyze rapid healing responses, and reduce the need for prescription drugs.

that patient's nausea following the procedure. That use of acupuncture fits very well the current model of how Western medicine views acupuncture. Western medicine thinks that only surgery, chemotherapy, radiation and prescription drugs can do the "real work" of healing, and that acupuncture should only be used to treat secondary symptoms, such as pain or nausea that follow the radical procedures conducted by Western doctors.

This is a rather blatant marginalization of acupuncture, and it is the only way in which modern medicine feels comfortable to discuss acupuncture at all. If they can keep acupuncture trapped in a small box of so-called "approved uses," they can effectively marginalize this entire field of medicine and continue to rely on their own favorite procedures such as drugs and surgery. But the reality is that acupuncture has far greater potential than this.

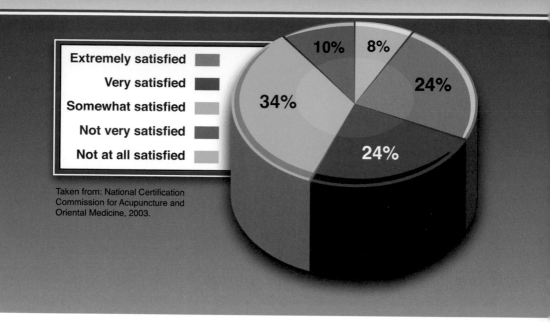

Extremely satisfied

Very satisfied

Somewhat satisfied

Not very satisfied

Not at all satisfied

8%

24%

24%

34%

10%

Taken from: National Certification
Commission for Acupuncture and
Oriental Medicine, 2003.

Powerful Potential

Acupuncture can treat patients in ways that can catalyze rapid healing responses. Acupuncture can often take the place of surgery or eliminate the need for prescription drugs. [It] . . . can treat a great many health disorders with tremendous success, and this is the truth about acupuncture that makes modern medicine extremely uncomfortable. Any time a complementary therapy begins to encroach upon the territory of more barbaric Western treatments, organized medicine starts to get a bit defensive. They don't want anything competing with their profit centers, which are, of course, prescription drugs, surgery, chemotherapy, and other such radical treatments.

So the official word that you are likely to hear about acupuncture for many years to come is that yes, it's fine for treating pain, or reducing nausea, or doing other minor things to help patients, but that if you're really sick, you should go get surgery, or you should start taking all of these prescription drugs for the rest of your life, or you should get chemotherapy that destroys your immune system.

That's going to continue to be the message from modern medicine for a while yet, until we get to a real revolution in healing and medicine. And once that revolution gains momentum, you will see acupuncture finally accepted in Western societies as a true healing therapy that has tremendous potential for enhancing the health of patients without dangerous side effects.

EVALUATING THE AUTHOR'S ARGUMENTS:

How would you describe the tone of the author's argument? How would you characterize his feelings toward modern medicine? What reason or reasons does he give for saying that modern medicine marginalizes acupuncture?

Acupuncture Is Ineffective

Stephen Barrett

"Acupuncture studies have shown that it makes no difference where you put the needles. Or whether you use needles or just pretend to use needles."

In the following viewpoint Stephen Barrett argues that acupuncture is a moneymaking scam. According to Barrett, studies using fake acupuncture needles prove that acupuncture does not provide any real healing benefits. Barrett questions the training and credentials of acupuncturists and calls their diagnoses, such as "Qi stagnation" or "blood stagnation," absurd. Barrett does not believe acupuncturists can properly diagnose real medical ailments. Barrett is a retired psychiatrist, author, and consumer advocate. Additionally, he is the head of the organization Quackwatch and is vice president of the National Council Against Health Fraud.

AS YOU READ, CONSIDER THE FOLLOWING QUESTIONS:

1. According to Barrett, what did two scientists at the University of Heidelberg develop that allowed researchers to conduct better-designed control studies?
2. According to the author, what caused the acupuncture boom in the United States in 1971?
3. Barrett explains that after attending a lecture in 1998 he was diagnosed by a practitioner of traditional Chinese medicine (TCM). What two things did the TCM practitioner do to diagnose Barrett?

Stephen Barrett, "Be Wary of Acupuncture, Qigong, and 'Chinese Medicine,'" *Quackwatch*, December 30, 2007. Reproduced by permission.

"Chinese medicine," often called "Oriental medicine" or "traditional Chinese medicine (TCM)," encompasses a vast array of folk medical practices based on mysticism. It holds that the body's vital energy (*chi* or *qi*) circulates through channels, called *meridians*, that have branches connected to bodily organs and functions. Illness is attributed to imbalance or interruption of *chi*. Ancient practices such as acupuncture, Qigong, and the use of various herbs are claimed to restore balance.

Traditional Acupuncture

Traditional acupuncture, as now practiced, involves the insertion of stainless steel needles into various body areas. A low-frequency current may be applied to the needles to produce greater stimulation. Other procedures used separately or together with acupuncture include: moxibustion (burning of floss or herbs applied to the skin); injection of sterile water, procaine, morphine, vitamins, or homeopathic solutions through the inserted needles; applications of laser beams (laserpuncture); placement of needles in the external ear (auriculotherapy); and acupressure (use of manual pressure). Treatment is applied to "acupuncture points," which are said to be located throughout the body. Originally there were 365 such points, corresponding to the days of the year, but the number identified by proponents during the past 2,000 years has increased gradually to about 2,000. Some practitioners place needles at or near the site of disease, whereas others select points on the basis of symptoms. In traditional acupuncture, a combination of points is usually used. . . .

Most acupuncturists espouse the traditional Chinese view of health and disease and consider acupuncture, herbal medicine, and related practices to be valid approaches to the full gamut of disease. Others reject the traditional approach and merely claim that acupuncture offers a simple way to achieve pain relief. The diagnostic process used by TCM practitioners may include questioning (medical history, lifestyle), observations (skin, tongue, color), listening (breathing sounds), and pulse-taking. Six pulse aspects said to correlate with body organs or functions are checked on each wrist to determine which meridians are "deficient" in *chi*. (Medical science recognizes only one pulse, corresponding to the heartbeat, which can be felt in the wrist, neck, feet, and various other places.) Some acupuncturists state that the electrical properties of the body may become imbalanced weeks or even months before symptoms occur. These practitioners claim that acupuncture can be used to treat conditions when the patient just "doesn't feel right," even though no disease is apparent.

TCM (as well as the folk medical practices of various other Asian countries) is a threat to certain animal species. For example, black bears—valued for their gall bladders [bear bile is thought to have healing properties]—have been hunted nearly to extinction in Asia, and poaching of black bears is a serious problem in North America.

Questionable Research

The conditions claimed to respond to acupuncture include chronic pain (neck and back pain, migraine headaches), acute injury-related pain (strains, muscle and ligament tears), gastrointestinal problems (indigestion, ulcers, constipation, diarrhea), cardiovascular conditions (high and low blood pressure), genitourinary problems (menstrual irregularity, frigidity, impotence), muscle and nerve conditions (paralysis, deafness), and behavioral problems (overeating, drug dependence, smoking). However, the evidence supporting these claims consists mostly of practitioners' observations and poorly designed studies. A controlled study found that electroacupuncture of the ear was no more effective than placebo stimulation (light touching) against chronic pain. In 1990, three Dutch epidemiologists analyzed 51 controlled studies of acupuncture for chronic pain and concluded that "the quality of even the better studies proved to be mediocre. . . . The efficacy of acupuncture in the treatment of chronic pain remains doubtful." They also examined reports of acupuncture used to treat addictions to cigarettes, heroin, and alcohol, and concluded that claims that acupuncture is effective as a therapy for these conditions are not supported by sound clinical research. . . .

The quality of TCM research in China has been extremely poor. A recent analysis of 2,938 reports of clinical trials reported in Chinese medical journals concluded that no conclusions could be drawn from the vast majority of them. . . .

Sham Acupuncture

Two scientists at the University of Heidelberg have developed a "fake needle" that may enable acupuncture researchers to perform better-

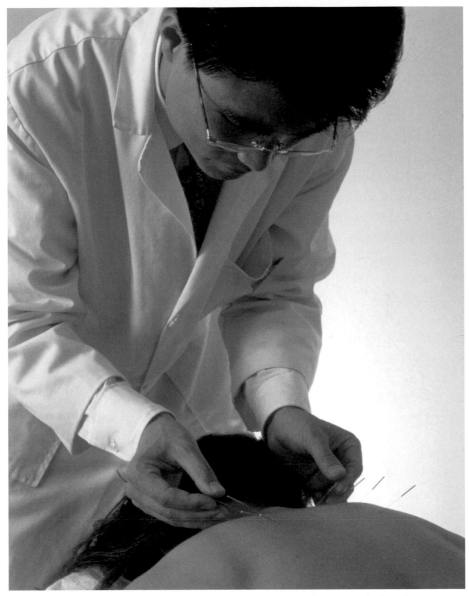

An acupuncturist inserts needles in a patient's back. The author contends that there is no difference where the needles are placed—in the end, it is "tooth fairy science."

designed controlled studies. The device is a needle with a blunt tip that moves freely within a copper handle. When the tip touches the skin, the patient feels a sensation similar to that of an acupuncture needle. At the same time, the visible part of the needle moves inside the handle so it appears to shorten as though penetrating the skin. When the device was tested on volunteers, none suspected that it had not penetrated the skin.

In 2004, a University of Heidelberg team proved the worth of their "sham acupuncture" technique in a study of postoperative nausea and vomiting (PONV) in women who underwent breast or gynecologic surgery. The study involved 220 women who received either acupuncture or the sham procedure at the acupuncture point "Pericardium 6" on the inside of the forearm. No significant difference in PONV or antivomiting medication use was found between the two groups or between the people who received treatment before anesthesia was induced and those who received it while anesthetized. A subgroup analysis found that vomiting was "significantly reduced" among the acupuncture patients, but the authors correctly noted that this finding might be due to studying multiple outcomes. (As the number of different outcome measures increases, so do the odds that a "statistically significant" finding will be spurious.) This study is important because PONV reduction is one of the few alleged benefits of acupuncture supported by reports in scientific journals. However, the other positive studies were not as tightly controlled.

Harriet Hall, a retired family practitioner who is interested in quackery, has summed up the significance of acupuncture research in an interesting way:

> Acupuncture studies have shown that it makes no difference where you put the needles. Or whether you use needles or just pretend to use needles (as long as the subject believes you used them). Many acupuncture researchers are doing what I call Tooth Fairy science: measuring how much money is left under the pillow without bothering to ask if the Tooth Fairy is real.

Improperly performed acupuncture can cause fainting, local hematoma (due to bleeding from a punctured blood vessel), pneumothorax (punctured lung), convulsions, local infections, hepatitis B (from unsterile needles), bacterial endocarditis, contact dermatitis, and nerve damage. The herbs used by acupuncture practitioners are not regulated for safety, potency, or effectiveness. There is also risk that an acupuncturist whose approach to diagnosis is not based on scientific concepts will fail to diagnose a dangerous condition. . . .

Meaningless Credentials

In 1971, an acupuncture boom occurred in the United States because of stories about visits to China by various American dignitaries. Entrepreneurs, both medical and nonmedical, began using flamboyant advertising techniques to promote clinics, seminars, demonstrations, books, correspondence courses, and do-it-yourself kits. Today some states restrict the practice of acupuncture to physicians or others operating under their direct supervision. In about 20 states, people who lack medical training can perform acupuncture without medical supervision. . . .

The National Certification Commission for Acupuncture and Oriental Medicine (NCCAOM) has set voluntary certification standards and offers separate certifications on Oriental medicine, acupuncture, Chinese herbology, and Asian bodywork therapy. In 2007, it reported that its certification programs or exams were [to] be recognized for licensure in 40 states and the District of Columbia and that more than 20,000 practitioners are licensed in the United States. . . .

> **FAST FACT**
>
> According to *Acupuncture Today*, as of September 30, 2008, there were 16,324 acupuncturists in the United States, and 6,024 were in California alone.

The credentials used by acupuncturists include C.A. (certified acupuncturist), Lic. Ac. (licensed acupuncturist), M.A. (master acupuncturist), Dip. Ac. (diplomate of acupuncture), Dipl. O.M. (diplomate of Oriental medicine), and O.M.D. (doctor of Oriental medicine). Some of these have legal significance, but they do not signify that the holder is competent to make adequate diagnoses or render appropriate treatment.

In 1990, the U.S. Secretary of Education recognized what is now called the Accreditation Commission for Acupuncture and Oriental Medicine (ACAOM) as an accrediting agency. However, such recognition is not based on the scientific validity of what is taught but upon other criteria. [Psychiatrist] George A. Ulett has noted:

> Certification of acupuncturists is a sham. While a few of those so accredited are naive physicians, most are nonmedical persons

Real Acupuncture Is No Different than Sham Acupuncture

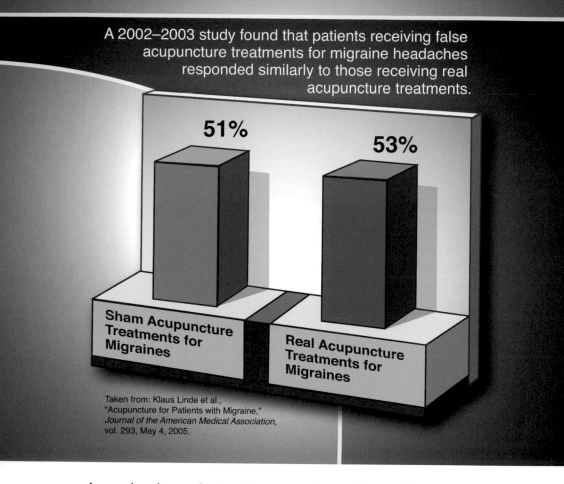

A 2002–2003 study found that patients receiving false acupuncture treatments for migraine headaches responded similarly to those receiving real acupuncture treatments.

51%

53%

Sham Acupuncture Treatments for Migraines

Real Acupuncture Treatments for Migraines

Taken from: Klaus Linde et al., "Acupuncture for Patients with Migraine," *Journal of the American Medical Association*, vol. 293, May 4, 2005.

who only play at being doctor and use this certification as an umbrella for a host of unproven New Age hokum treatments. Unfortunately, a few HMOs, hospitals, and even medical schools are succumbing to the bait and exposing patients to such bogus treatments when they need real medical care.

The National Council Against Health Fraud has concluded:
• Acupuncture is an unproven modality of treatment.
• Its theory and practice are based on primitive and fanciful concepts of health and disease that bear no relationship to present scientific knowledge.

- Research during the past 20 years has not demonstrated that acupuncture is effective against any disease.
- Perceived effects of acupuncture are probably due to a combination of expectation, suggestion, counter-irritation, conditioning, and other psychologic mechanisms.
- The use of acupuncture should be restricted to appropriate research settings.
- Insurance companies should not be required by law to cover acupuncture treatment.
- Licensure of lay acupuncturists should be phased out.
- Consumers who wish to try acupuncture should discuss their situation with a knowledgeable physician who has no commercial interest. . . .

Dubious Diagnoses

In 1998, following a lecture I attended at a local college, an experienced TCM practitioner diagnosed me by taking my pulse and looking at my tongue. He stated that my pulse showed signs of "stress" and that my tongue indicated I was suffering from "congestion of the blood." A few minutes later, he told a woman that her pulse showed premature ventricular contractions (a disturbance of the heart's rhythm that could be harmless or significant, depending on whether the individual has underlying heart disease). He suggested that both of us undergo treatment with acupuncture and herbs—which would have cost about $90 per visit. I took the woman's pulse and found that it was completely normal. I believe that the majority of nonmedical acupuncturists rely on improper diagnostic procedures. . . .

A study published in 2001 illustrates the absurdity of TCM practices. A 40-year-old woman with chronic back pain who visited seven acupuncturists during a two-week period was diagnosed with "Qi stagnation" by 6 of them, "blood stagnation" by 5, "kidney Qi deficiency" by 2, "yin deficiency" by 1, and "liver Qi deficiency" by 1. The proposed treatments varied even more. Among the six who recorded their recommendations, the practitioners planned to use between 7 and 26 needles inserted into 4 to 16 specific "acupuncture points" in the back, leg, hand, and foot. Of 28 acupuncture points selected, only 4 (14%) were prescribed by two or more acupuncturists. The study appears to have been designed to make the results as consistent as possible. All of the acupuncturists had been trained at a school of traditional Chinese medicine (TCM). Six other volunteers were excluded because they "used highly atypical practices," and three were excluded because they had been in practice for less than three years. Whereas science-based methods are thoroughly studied to ensure that they are reliable, this appears to be the first published study that examines the consistency of TCM diagnosis or treatment. I would expect larger studies to show that TCM diagnoses are meaningless and have little or nothing to do with the patient's health status. The study's authors state that the diagnostic findings showed "considerable consistency" because nearly all of the practitioners found Qi or blood stagnation. However, the most likely explanation is that these are diagnosed in nearly everyone. It would be fascinating to see what would happen if a healthy person was examined by multiple acupuncturists.

EVALUATING THE AUTHOR'S ARGUMENTS:

Authors use different methods to support their viewpoints, including statistics, expert opinions, or anecdotes. Which methods does Stephen Barrett use to support his viewpoint?

Homeopathy Is Effective

Carolyn Dean and Elissa Meininger

"The very symptoms that allopaths suppress are the ones the body uses to get well and that a homeopath surveys to find the appropriate remedy to help the body heal."

In the following viewpoint Carolyn Dean and Elissa Meininger contend that homeopathic medicine is superior to allopathic medicine. Homeopathic medicine is based on the belief that natural substances, prepared in a special way, can treat medical ailments. This contrasts with allopathic medicine, also called Western medicine, modern medicine, or mainstream medicine, with which medical doctors treat symptoms and diseases primarily using drugs, radiation, or surgery. Dean and Meininger tell the story behind homeopathy, starting over one hundred years ago when it challenged the theories of allopathic medicine. According to Dean and Meininger, when homeopathy first came to the United States, it was very popular. It was so popular that doctors espousing allopathic medicine recognized the competition and felt threatened by it. Subsequently, they mounted a successful attack on homeopathy, causing its popularity to dwindle. Dean and Meininger believe that homeopathy is a superior form of treatment and that someday it will reemerge to challenge allopathic medicine. Dean is a medical and naturopathic doctor, herbalist, acupuncturist, nutrition-ist, the president of Friends of Freedom International, and an author. Meininger is the vice president of Friends of Freedom International, cofounder of the Health Freedom Action Network, and the host of a natural-health radio show in Oklahoma City. The article is available online at www.newswithviews.com/Dean/carolyn29.htm.

AS YOU READ, CONSIDER THE FOLLOWING QUESTIONS:
1. What do the authors identify as the homeland of homeopathy?
2. According to Dean and Meininger, who is the "father" of homeopathy?
3. What old idea does the "law of similars" come from, according to the authors?

In America and in the West, the public is conditioned to believe that modern (allopathic) medicine is the supreme healing modal-ity. Propaganda machines that rely on media in need of content and not necessarily truth eagerly spread this notion. Scientific journal articles promoting drugs are little more than press releases by phar-maceutical companies signed by doctors for hire. In the midst of the recent "outing" of unsafe drugs by whistleblowers; the thousands of law suits against drug companies for drug damage; and a plethora of books and articles enumerating the side effects of drugs and the hundreds of thousands of lives lost we see drug companies and the WTO determined to control dietary supplements through Codex and international trade agreements in their global quest for power.

Why is this happening? Simply because most of the world does not use modern medicine and the powers that be want to control those other forms of medicine to make way for a seamless, worldwide assembly line–style of health delivery by government decree favor-ing the highly-profitable, patented products and services of modern (allopathic) medicine.

One of the forms of medicine that is being targeted for control is homeopathy—the topic of this week's column. Both Elissa and I have a deep and abiding love of homeopathy and we speak up for it whenever we can.

Homeopathy is one of those systems of medicine that is all encompassing and could be a life-long project of study. I wanted to make it my prime modality after medical school and began learning it during my naturopathic training. That might have had something to do with genes because my grandmother was a nurse and a homeopath. And my father, while still in high school, was on the lists to enter Boston University School of Medicine, which, at the time, was a homeopathic medical school. I found, however, that I'm much too eclectic to stay in one place for too long. But I stayed long enough to see some miraculous cures take place. In the hands of a skilled homeopath, it is one of the best existing modalities for all conditions. I recommend it to parents as the best form of medicine for children and the best for most acute conditions and advise people to have a homeopathic kit on hand to treat emergencies.

Elissa's reasons are even more personal. After a lifetime of ill health due to a missed diagnosis of mercury poisoning from her dental fillings (a disease that is not recognized by either the American dental community or modern [allopathic] medicine), Elissa was diagnosed by a homeopath and from the first dose of a homeopathic remedy, she found her salvation. Up until then, she had experienced not just debilitating symptoms of serious chronic illness, but numerous extreme adverse reactions from such things as penicillin and Tylenol. To find out why she was misdiagnosed all those years and why she was never referred to homeopathy, a medical philosophy that has specialized in the diagnosis and treatment of medically-induced mercury poisoning for 200 years, prompted Elissa to become the health policy expert she is today. She earned her expertise by delving into the depth and breadth of the history of American medicine and how politics and the clever actions of several self-interest groups, over time, created today's modern medical monopoly folly.

The story of how homeopathy first came to America, became the second most practiced healing art by public demand, and then was virtually destroyed by Big Pharma and its allies, the AMA and the practitioners of modern (allopathic) medicine, is why we have called our article "The Worst Crime of the 20th Century." This history bears witness to how the self-interest of just a handful of people, by creating an allopathic medical monopoly, continues to cause the needless deaths of millions of people and the ongoing suffering of millions more.

As the story goes, back in the mid-1800s, homeopathy had arrived on our shores from its homeland, Germany, and the public eagerly flocked to homeopathic physicians. And no wonder. The "modern (allopathic) medicine" of the day included draining people of up to 32 ounces of blood and dosing them with lethal amounts of mercury in a product called "calomel." Calomel caused profuse salivation and doctors measured the amount of saliva by the pint as a means of determining the success of the treatment. Calomel was considered the all-purpose elixir for most ailments along with the bleeding, so you can see why homeopathy spread rapidly. Homeopaths found allopathic treatment barbaric.

The cholera epidemics of the nineteenth century provided proof that homeopathic treatments were more successful at combating the disease than traditional allopathic medicine.

What confounded the practitioners of "modern (allopathic) medicine" of that era was that homeopaths were well-educated and had quickly fallen into favor with the educated, politically powerful and wealthier clientele, as well as the masses. Worse yet, while their medical philosophy confounded the average practitioner of "modern (allopathic) medicine," every time an allopath actually took an honest look at how homeopathy was practiced, another convert to homeopathy was born. In fact, in many cases, practicing homeopaths were actually converts from "modern (allopathic) medicine."

Proof that homeopathy worked was widespread. Every epidemic in Europe and America starting with the cholera epidemics in the 1840s became an advertisement for the virtues of homeopathy. Homeopaths saved lives in such large numbers and compared to the competition it was obvious that allopathic methods were a complete failure. In rapid order, the practice of homeopathy became widespread in New England, the Middle Atlantic States, and the Midwest. And, true to form, while the South had been slow to catch on, the 1878 yellow fever epidemic converted many patients and doctors there, too.

The formation of the American Medical Association in the 1840s was in direct response to the onslaught of a superior medical system. From the beginning, the AMA stood firm with a hostile "them or us" attitude about members consorting with the competition. Well-educated homeopaths, often graduates of Harvard, Yale and other such schools, were banned from joining the AMA. In AMA meetings, any discussion about homeopathy was banned. If any member of the AMA, or its state chapters, were seen consorting with a homeopath, that doctor was expelled.

Voluminous and vicious literature was written and circulated about the worthlessness of homeopathy. When the drug industry emerged as an economic force in the 1870s, flush with its profits from selling mercury medicinals to the Union Army, the AMA found the sugar daddy of its dreams that could fuel and finance an all out war against its most serious competition. This polemic propaganda continues today because the 1500 or so effective homeopathic remedies that have been developed over 200 years represent serious competition for Big Pharma. Furthermore, homeopathic remedies have proven to have no dangerous side effects, are not patentable, can be manufactured and sold for pennies and have a very long shelf life.

Those who practice medicine in the allopathic tradition, then as now, know instinctively that homeopathy, by its very principles, is a rejection of the assumptions held near and dear to modern medicine. In fact, it is important to know that homeopathy is actually the invention of a German medical genius named Samuel Hahnemann, and it comes from Hahnemann's rejection of what he was taught as an allopathic physician in his day, 200 years ago.

What Hahnemann saw was a failure to truly heal people. As a linguist with knowledge of many ancient and modern languages, including several from the Arab world, Hahnemann made a good deal of his living translating scientific and medical texts. This gave him access to some of the greatest minds in the world's medical traditions and it was when he was questioning the conclusions of British doctor, William Cullen, regarding the use of Peruvian bark to treat malaria, that Hahnemann experienced a flash of insight that fostered homeopathy.

FAST FACT

The market for vitamins, minerals, homeopathics, and herbals is expected to reach $8.5 billion by 2012, according to a study by market research firm Packaged Facts.

At the height of its popularity in America, homeopathy was second only to allopathy in the number of practitioners. It had its own schools, its own pharmacies and even had a monument erected to honor Hahnemann in Washington, D.C., considered by many to be one of the great geniuses in the history of medicine.

At the time this monument to Hahnemann was unveiled, there where 22 homeopathic medical schools in America. One of the more interesting ones was The New England Female College founded in 1850 as the world's first women's medical school. During its time, it graduated the first black woman doctor and after it was absorbed into Boston University to become Boston University Medical School in 1873, it became America's first coed medical school. In 1897, the new school graduated its first black doctor, who went on to become America's first black psychiatrist.

Ironically, four years after the monument was erected, and 10 years before the publication of the *Flexner Report,* the blueprint of the allopathic medical monopoly, the trustees of Boston University were told by AMA officials that if they didn't convert the medical school curricula to all-allopathic, their graduates would have difficulty taking and passing state medical licensing examinations. At the time, there were 645 practicing homeopaths in Boston alone.

So, what allopathic assumptions does homeopathy reject? At its core, homeopathy is based, not on a biochemical or mechanistic model like allopathy, but on the idea that each person has a vital force, a resonating frequency, if you will. This vital force, called Qi or Chi in Asian healing arts, is basically the energy or essence of the person that can be observed and measured. In the simplest terms, when you are ill, according to homeopathic philosophy, your frequency changes and symptoms occur as a result of your body trying to restore you to a healthy frequency. The symptoms serve as the means by which restoration of health can be achieved. The very symptoms that allopaths suppress are the ones the body uses to get well and that a homeopath surveys to find the appropriate remedy to help the body heal.

To a homeopath, an office call is basically devoted to systematically interviewing the patient to determine what makes them tick as well as gathering as much information about each of their symptoms as possible. Then, after analyzing this information, the homeopath has available 1500 or so catalogued remedies that are inventoried according to symptoms and constitution.

The information in these reference manuals is drawn from data on literally thousands of patients who have been treated successfully. Homeopathic remedies themselves are developed by a process called "potentization" which renders them not only non-toxic but leaves only a minute vibration in the water of the original substance. These potentized remedies, when they enter the person's body as a frequency, not a chemical substance, basically help revitalize the person's own harmonious frequency.

To modern (allopathic) medical practitioners, a symptom is a bad outcome of an illness and suppressing the symptom is the first thing a doctor tries to do to make the patient feel better. Suppression of symptoms is not the same as healing the person.

Each homeopathic remedy is developed by first testing it on healthy people based on an idea called "the law of similars." The law of similars comes from an old idea that a substance that can create a symptom in a healthy person can cure a sick person suffering the same symptom. The law of similars confounds the scientific assumptions of the biochemically-based allopathic medical community and until you experience the healing process yourself, you will probably scratch your head, wondering what these homeopaths are talking about. Hahnemann came to name his new school of thought homeo (Greek for "similar"), pathy (Greek for "suffering). He then named the old school of thought allo (Greek for "other"), pathy.

These opposing views on the meaning of symptoms and what a doctor does about them is the sharpest of many ideological divisions between homeopathy and allopathy.

For most of the 1800s, allopaths were called allopaths but when the AMA orchestrated the publication of the *Flexner Report* in 1910, to outline their new medical monopoly, the first order of business was to make sure the word "allopathy" no longer defined them. They wanted ALL practitioners of all "cults" or "dogmas" as they insultingly referred to their competition, to give up their differing medical ideas and "surrender" to modern science.

The *Flexner Report* was used to convince the financial backers of non-allopathic medical schools, particularly homeopathy, to cease providing funding. Within 20 years, all but one homeopathic school had been closed or forced to convert to allopathic teaching only.

It came to our attention within the last week or so, that Citizens for Health, one of the major national health freedom groups, in conjunction with the National Center for Homeopathy, had organized a writing campaign to the CDC to include homeopathic research as part of its agenda for the next decade. [homeopathic.org/]

This campaign, with the deadline of January 15, 2006, is now over. However, we have mixed feelings about how the modern medicine dominated CDC, or the NIH or any other of the usual research organizations could possibly conduct honest and relevant research on homeopathy, given the fact that modern medicine is based on such vastly different assumptions.

We also have concerns because of recent revelations about the corruption in science in all venues as well as the faking of scientific papers being published in prestigious medical journals. We have concerns

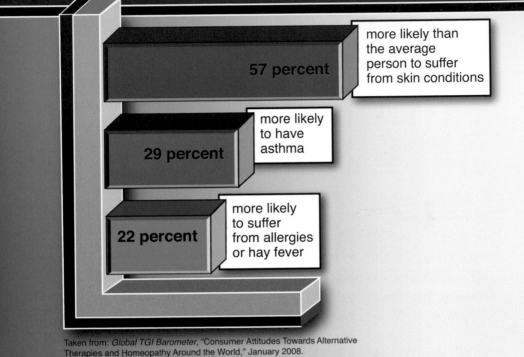

Consumer Attitudes Toward Homeopathic Medicine

Homeopathic Medicine Advocates in the United States Are:

57 percent more likely than the average person to suffer from skin conditions

29 percent more likely to have asthma

22 percent more likely to suffer from allergies or hay fever

Taken from: *Global TGI Barometer*, "Consumer Attitudes Towards Alternative Therapies and Homeopathy Around the World," January 2008.

about the political and economic agendas of those in control of directing what research shall be done and that, somehow, homeopathy will be tainted keeping it in the same false and negative light it has been held for most of the 20th century.

We suggest that there are ample books written by practicing homeopaths about the success of homeopathy for any open-minded person to see its worth. In any case, we are foursquare behind restoring homeopathy to its former position as the second largest medical system in America and give you practical resources at the end to pursue your own investigation of homeopathy.

To sum up the worldview on homeopathy we recently read an article in the *New India Press*, dated December 24, 2005, titled, "WHO Recognition for Homeopathy." We thought you might like to read some excerpts from this article to give you a flavor of how homeopathy is discussed in a country where it is widely accepted and used.

"Deviating from the trend of rejecting homeopathy treatment and medicine as mere placebos, the World Health Organization (WHO) has declared that homeopathy is the second-most used medical system internationally.

"Clinical trials have proved that this method of treatment has been successful if the practitioners have taken into account the individual holistic nature of the patient before opting for homeopathy." Says Dr. T N Sreedhara Kurup, Assistant Director In-Charge of the Central Research Institute for Homeopathy.

"Different patients will receive different treatments for the same disease making it difficult to conduct randomised control trials," he said. "Homeopathy is that stream of medicine, which prescribes medicines suitable to the individual and the cost of treatment is affordable when compared to Allopathy. Besides, it is claimed that homeopathic medicines are devoid of any harmful side-effects," says Dr. Ravi M Nair, a homeopathy specialist.

In all, the *New India Press* estimates that "about 500 million people rely on homeopathy treatment in the world. As a system of medicine, it draws support from hundreds of thousands of doctors, teaching institutions and universities where homeopathy is taught."

We conclude that as allopathic medicine is relegated to its proper place—surgery and emergency medicine, homeopathy and other natural healing arts will once again flourish and inspire.

Resources:
http://www.homeopathic.com/
http://www.healthyhomeopathy.com/

Act for Health Freedom Now:
Go to www.friendsoffreedominternational.org view and purchase the new movie on Codex and Free Trade called "We Become Silent" by Kevin Miller.

Also purchase "Death by Modern Medicine." Proceeds from the sale of these products are crucial to help us fund our health freedom action. For state action go to: www.nationalhealthfreedom.org.

EVALUATING THE AUTHORS' ARGUMENTS:

In this viewpoint the authors argue that homeopathy is superior to allopathy by telling the history of homeopathic medicine in the United States. Do you think knowing the story behind homeopathy coming to the United States is effective in making their point? Why or why not?

Homeopathy Is Ineffective

Ben Goldacre

"People getting the placebo sugar pills do just as well as those getting the real, posh, expensive, technical, magical, homeopathy pills."

In the following viewpoint Ben Goldacre argues that homeopathic remedies are no more effective than sugar pills. He says the homeopathic industry tries to do everything it can to hide this fact, but the evidence shows that homeopathic remedies do not work. Goldacre says that it is absurd to think that anything diluted almost to infinity, as homeopathic remedies are, can cure anything. Goldacre is a doctor and author. He writes a regular column for the *Guardian* called Bad Science.

AS YOU READ, CONSIDER THE FOLLOWING QUESTIONS:

1. According to Goldacre, what book contains a reference to the first randomized control trial and what was tested?
2. What does Goldacre say is a "meta-analysis"?
3. According to Goldacre, what does Peter Chappell claim to have done?

The following correction was printed in the *Guardian*'s Corrections and Clarifications column, Monday December 10 2007:

The comment piece below responded in part to an earlier article by Jeanette Winterson: In defence of homeopathy, and referred to her view that there is a role for homeopathy in the treatment of HIV in Africa. Jeanette Winterson has asked us to make clear, in case there is any doubt, that she does not believe that homeopathy can replace anti-retroviral drugs (ARVs) and she does not support homeopaths who make claims that may deter those with HIV from taking ARVs.

There are some aspects of quackery that are harmless—childish even—and there are some that are very serious indeed. On Tuesday, to my great delight, the author Jeanette Winterson launched a scientific defence of homeopathy in these pages. She used words such as "nano" meaninglessly, she suggested that there is a role for homeopathy in the treatment of HIV in Africa, and she said that an article in the Lancet today will call on doctors to tell their patients that homeopathic "medicines" offer no benefit.

The article does not say that, and I should know, because I wrote it. It is not an act of fusty authority, and I claim none: I look about 12, and I'm only a few years out of medical school. This is all good fun, but my adamant stance, that I absolutely lack any authority, is key: because this is not about one man's opinion, and there is nothing even slightly technical or complicated about the evidence on homeopathy, or indeed anything, when it is clearly explained.

And there is the rub. Because Winterson tries to tell us—like every other homeopathy fan—that for some mystical reason, which is never made entirely clear, the healing powers of homeopathic pills are special, and so their benefits cannot be tested like every other pill. This has become so deeply embedded in our culture, by an industry eager to obscure our very understanding of evidence, that even some doctors now believe it.

Enough is enough. Evidence-based medicine is beautiful, elegant, clever and, most of all, important. It is how we know what will kill or cure you. These are biblical themes, and it is ridiculous that what

I am going to explain to you now is not taught in schools. So let's imagine that we are talking to a fan of homeopathy, one who is both intelligent and reflective. "Look," they begin, "all I know is that I feel better when I take a homeopathic pill." OK, you reply. We absolutely accept that. Nobody can take that away from the homeopathy fan.

But perhaps it's the placebo effect? You both think you know about the placebo effect already, but you are both wrong. The mysteries of the interaction between body and mind are far more complex than can ever be permitted in the crude, mechanistic and reductionist world of the alternative therapist, where pills do all the work.

The placebo response is about far more than the pills—it is about the cultural meaning of a treatment, our expectation, and more. So we know that four sugar pills a day will clear up ulcers quicker than two sugar pills, we know that a saltwater injection is a more effective treatment for pain than a sugar pill, we know that green sugar pills are more effective for anxiety than red, and we know that brand packaging on painkillers increases pain relief.

A baby will respond to its parents' expectations and behaviour, and the placebo effect is still perfectly valid for children and pets. Placebo pills with no active ingredient can even elicit measurable biochemical responses in humans, and in animals (when they have come to associate the pill with an active ingredient). This is undoubtedly one of the most interesting areas of medical science ever.

"Well, it could be that," says your honest, reflective homeopathy fan. "I have no way of being certain. But I just don't think that's it. All I know is, I get better with homeopathy."

Ah, now, but could that be because of "regression to the mean"? This is an even more fascinating phenomenon: all things, as the new-agers like to say, have a natural cycle. Your back pain goes up and down over a week, or a month, or a year. Your mood rises and falls. That weird lump in your wrist comes and goes. You get a cold; it gets better.

If you take an ineffective sugar pill, at your sickest, it's odds on you're going to get better, in exactly the same way that if you sacrifice a goat, after rolling a double six, your next roll is likely to be lower. That is regression to the mean.

"Well, it could be that," says the homeopathy fan. "But I just don't think so. All I know is, I get better with homeopathy."

The author argues that homeopathic remedies are no more effective than placebos (pictured), and there has not been much information on the overall effects of homeopathy.

How can you both exclude these explanations—since you both need to—and move on from this impasse? Luckily homeopaths have made a very simple, clear claim: they say that the pill they prescribe will make you get better.

You could do a randomised, controlled trial on almost any intervention you wanted to assess: comparing two teaching methods, or two forms of psychotherapy, or two plant-growth boosters—literally anything. The first trial was in the Bible (Daniel 1: 1-16, since you asked) and compared the effect of two different diets on soldiers' vigour. Doing a trial is not a new or complicated idea, and a pill is the easiest thing to test of all.

Here is a model trial for homeopathy. You take, say, 200 people, and divide them at random into two groups of 100. All of the patients visit their homeopath, they all get a homeopathic prescription at the end (because homeopaths love to prescribe pills even more than doctors) for whatever it is that the homeopath wants to prescribe, and all the patients take their prescription to the homeopathic pharmacy. Every patient can be prescribed something completely different, an "individualised" prescription—it doesn't matter.

Now here is the twist: one group gets the real homeopathy pills they were prescribed (whatever they were), and the patients in the other group are given fake sugar pills. Crucially, neither the patients, nor the people who meet them in the trial, know who is getting which treatment.

This trial has been done, time and time again, with homeopathy, and when you do a trial like this, you find, overall, that the people getting the placebo sugar pills do just as well as those getting the real, posh, expensive, technical, magical homeopathy pills.

So how come you keep hearing homeopaths saying that there are trials where homeopathy does do better than placebo? This is where it gets properly interesting. This is where we start to see homeopaths, and indeed all alternative therapists more than ever, playing the same sophisticated tricks that big pharma still sometimes uses to pull the wool over the eyes of doctors.

Yes, there are some individual trials where homeopathy does better, first because there are a lot of trials that are simply not "fair tests". For example—and I'm giving you the most basic examples here—there are many trials in alternative therapy journals where the patients were not "blinded": that is, the patients knew whether they were getting the real treatment or the placebo. These are much more likely to be positive in favour of your therapy, for obvious reasons. There is no point in doing a trial if it is not a fair test: it ceases to be a trial, and simply becomes a marketing ritual.

There are also trials where it seems patients were not randomly allocated to the "homeopathy" or "sugar pill" groups: these are even sneakier. You should randomise patients by sealed envelopes with random numbers in them, opened only after the patient is fully registered into the trial. Let's say that you are "randomly allocating" patients by, um, well, the first patient gets homeopathy, then the next patient gets the sugar pills, and so on. If you do that, then you already know, as the person seeing the patient, which treatment they are going to get, before you decide whether or not they are suitable to be recruited into your trial. So a homeopath sitting in a clinic would be able—let's say unconsciously—to put more sick patients into the sugar pill group, and healthier patients into the homeopathy group, thus massaging the results. This, again, is not a fair test.

Congratulations. You now understand evidence-based medicine to degree level.

So when doctors say that a trial is weak, and poor quality, it's not because they want to maintain the hegemony, or because they work for "the man": it's because a poor trial is simply not a fair test of a treatment. And it's not cheaper to do a trial badly, it's just stupid, or, of course, conniving, since unfair tests will give false positives in favour of homeopathy.

Now there are bad trials in medicine, of course, but here's the difference: in medicine there is a strong culture of critical self-appraisal. Doctors are taught to spot bad research (as I am teaching you now) and bad drugs. The British Medical Journal recently published a list of the top three most highly accessed and referenced studies from the past year, and they were on, in order: the dangers of the anti-inflammatory Vioxx; the problems with the antidepressant paroxetine; and the dangers of SSRI antidepressants in general. This is as it should be.

With alternative therapists, when you point out a problem with the evidence, people don't engage with you about it, or read and reference your work. They get into a huff. They refuse to answer calls or email queries. They wave their hands and mutter sciencey words such as "quantum" and "nano". They accuse you of being a paid plant from some big pharma conspiracy. They threaten to sue you. They shout, "What about thalidomide, science boy?", they cry, they call you names, they hold lectures at their trade fairs about how you are a dangerous doctor, they contact and harass your employer, they try to dig up dirt from your personal life, or they actually threaten you with violence (this has all happened to me, and I'm compiling a great collection of stories for a nice documentary, so do keep it coming).

But back to the important stuff. Why else might there be plenty of positive trials around, spuriously? Because of something called "publication bias". In all fields of science, positive results are more likely to get published, because they are more newsworthy, there's more mileage in publishing them for your career, and they're more fun to write up. This is a problem for all of science. Medicine has addressed this problem, making people register their trial before they start, on a "clinical trials database", so that you cannot hide disappointing data and pretend it never happened.

How big is the problem of publication bias in alternative medicine? Well now, in 1995, only 1% of all articles published in alternative medicine journals gave a negative result. The most recent figure is 5% negative. This is very, very low.

There is only one conclusion you can draw from this observation. Essentially, when a trial gives a negative result, alternative therapists, homeopaths or the homeopathic companies simply do not publish it. There will be desk drawers, box files, computer folders, garages, and back offices filled with untouched paperwork on homeopathy trials that did not give the result the homeopaths wanted. At least one homeopath reading this piece will have a folder just like that, containing disappointing, unpublished data that they are keeping jolly quiet about. Hello there!

Now, you could just pick out the positive trials, as homeopaths do, and quote only those. This is called "cherry picking" the literature—it is not a new trick, and it is dishonest, because it misrepresents the totality of the literature. There is a special mathematical tool called a "meta-analysis", where you take all the results from all the studies on one subject, and put the figures into one giant spreadsheet, to get the most representative overall answer. When you do this, time and time again, and you exclude the unfair tests, and you account for publication bias, you find, in all homeopathy trials overall, that homeopathy does no better than placebos.

The preceding paragraphs took only three sentences in my brief Lancet piece, although only because that readership didn't need to be told what a meta-analysis is. Now, here is the meat. Should we even care, I asked, if homeopathy is no better than placebo? Because the strange answer is, maybe not.

Let me tell you about a genuine medical conspiracy to suppress alternative therapies. During the 19th-century cholera epidemic, death rates at the London Homeopathic Hospital were three times lower than at the Middlesex Hospital. Homeopathic sugar pills won't do anything against cholera, of course, but the reason for homeopathy's success in this epidemic is even more interesting than the placebo effect: at the time, nobody could treat cholera. So, while hideous medical treatments such as blood-letting were actively harmful, the homeopaths' treatments at least did nothing either way.

Today, similarly, there are often situations where people want treatment, but where medicine has little to offer—lots of back pain, stress at work, medically unexplained fatigue, and most common colds, to give just a few examples. Going through a theatre of medical treatment, and trying every medication in the book, will give you only side-effects. A sugar pill in these circumstances seems a very sensible option.

But just as homeopathy has unexpected benefits, so it can have unexpected side-effects. Prescribing a pill carries its own risks: it medicalises problems, it can reinforce destructive beliefs about illness, and it can promote the idea that a pill is an appropriate response to a social problem, or a modest viral illness.

But there are also ethical problems. In the old days, just 50 years ago, "communication skills" at medical school consisted of how not to tell your patient they had terminal cancer. Now doctors are very open and honest with their patients. When a healthcare practitioner of any description prescribes a pill that they know full well is no more effective than a placebo—without disclosing that fact to their patient—then they trample all over some very important modern ideas, such as getting informed consent from your patient, and respecting their autonomy.

Sure, you could argue that it might be in a patient's interest to lie to them, and I think there is an interesting discussion to be had here, but at least be aware that this is the worst kind of old-fashioned, Victorian doctor paternalism: and ultimately, when you get into the habit of misleading people, that undermines the relationship between all doctors and patients, which is built on trust, and ultimately honesty. If, on the other hand, you prescribe homeopathy pills, but you don't know that they perform any better than placebo in trials, then you are not familiar with the trial literature, and you are therefore incompetent to prescribe them. These are fascinating ethical problems, and yet I have never once found a single homeopath discussing them.

There are also more concrete harms. It's routine marketing practice for homeopaths to denigrate mainstream medicine. There's a simple commercial reason for this: survey data show that a disappointing experience with mainstream medicine is almost the only factor that regularly correlates with choosing alternative therapies. That's an explanation, but not an excuse. And this is not just talking medicine down. One study found that more than half of all the homeopaths approached advised patients against the MMR vaccine for their children, acting irresponsibly on what will quite probably come to be known as the media's MMR hoax. How did the alternative therapy world deal with this concerning finding, that so many among them were quietly undermining the vaccination schedule? Prince Charles's office tried to have the lead researcher sacked. A BBC Newsnight investigation found that almost all the homeopaths approached recommended ineffective homeopathic pills to protect against malaria, and advised against medical malaria prophylactics, while not even giving basic advice on bite prevention. Very holistic. Very "complementary". Any action against the homeopaths concerned? None.

And in the extreme, when they're not undermining public-health campaigns and leaving their patients exposed to fatal diseases, homeopaths who are not medically qualified can miss fatal diagnoses, or actively disregard them, telling their patients grandly to stop their inhalers, and throw away their heart pills. The Society of Homeopaths is holding a symposium on the treatment of Aids, featuring the work of Peter Chappell, a man who claims to have found a homeopathic solution to the epidemic. We reinforce all of this by collectively humouring homeopaths' healer fantasies, and by allowing them to tell porkies about evidence.

And what porkies. Somehow, inexplicably, a customer satisfaction survey from a homeopathy clinic is promoted in the media as if it trumps a string of randomised trials. No wonder the public find it

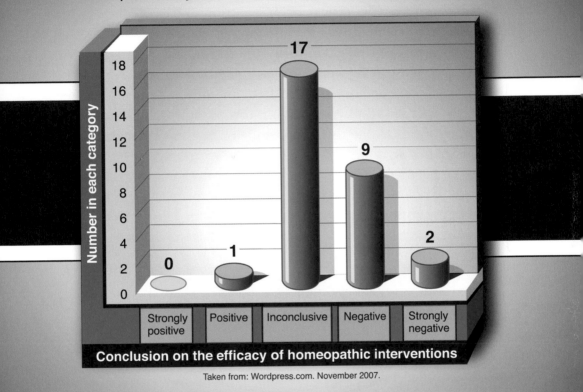

Most Research Results Listed for Homeopathy Are Inconclusive or Negative

The following is an assessment of the items of "evidence" listed for homeopathy in the British National Library for Health's "Complementary and Alternative Medicine Specialist Library."

Taken from: Wordpress.com. November 2007.

hard to understand medical research. Almost every time you read about a "trial" in the media, it is some bogus fish oil "trial" that isn't really a "trial", or a homeopath waving their hands about, because the media finds a colourful quack claim more interesting than genuine, cautious, bland, plodding medical research.

By pushing their product relentlessly with this scientific flim-flam, homeopaths undermine the public understanding of what it means to have an evidence base for a treatment. Worst of all, they do this at the very time when academics are working harder than ever to engage the public in a genuine collective ownership and understanding of clinical research, and when most good doctors are trying to educate and involve their patients in the selection of difficult treatment options. This is not a nerdy point. This is vital.

Here is the strangest thing. Every single criticism I have made could easily be managed with clear and open discussion of the problems. But homoeopaths have walled themselves off from the routine cut-and-thrust of academic medicine, and reasoned critique is all too often met with anger, shrieks of persecution and avoidance rather than argument. The Society of Homeopaths (the largest professional body in Europe, the ones running that frightening conference on HIV) have even threatened to sue bloggers who criticise them. The university courses on homeopathy that I and others have approached have flatly refused to provide basic information, such as what they teach and how. It's honestly hard to think of anything more unhealthy in an academic setting.

This is exactly what I said, albeit in nerdier academic language, in today's edition of the Lancet, Britain's biggest medical journal. These views are what homeopaths are describing as an "attack". But I am very clear. There is no single right way to package up all of this undeniable and true information into a "view" on homeopathy. When I'm feeling generous, I think: homeopathy could have value as placebo, on the NHS even, although there are ethical considerations, and these serious cultural side-effects to be addressed. But when they're suing people instead of arguing with them, telling people not to take their medical treatments, killing patients, running conferences on HIV fantasies, undermining the public's understanding of evidence and, crucially, showing absolutely no sign of ever being able to engage in a sensible conversation about the perfectly simple ethical and cultural problems that their practice faces, I think: these people are just morons. I can't help that: I'm human. The facts are sacred, but my view on them changes from day to day. And the only people who could fix me in one camp or the other, now, are the homeopaths themselves.

It Doesn't All Add Up . . . the 'Science' Behind Homeopathy

Homeopathic remedies are made by taking an ingredient, such as arsenic, and diluting it down so far that there is not a single molecule left in the dose that you get. The ingredients are selected on the basis of like cures like, so that a substance that causes sweating at normal doses, for example, would be used to treat sweating.

Many people confuse homeopathy with herbalism and do not realise just how far homeopathic remedies are diluted. The typical dilution is called "30C": this means that the original substance has been diluted by 1 drop in 100, 30 times. On the Society of Homeopaths site, in their "What is homeopathy?" section, they say that "30C contains less than 1 part per million of the original substance."

This is an understatement: a 30C homeopathic preparation is a dilution of 1 in 100^{30}, or rather 1 in 10^{60}, which means a 1 followed by 60 zeroes, or—let's be absolutely clear—a dilution of 1 in 1,000,000,000,000,000,000,000,000,000,000,000,000,000,000,0 00,000,000,000,000,000.

To phrase that in the Society of Homeopaths' terms, we should say: "30C contains less than one part per million million million million million million million million million million of the original substance."

At a homeopathic dilution of 100C, which they sell routinely, and which homeopaths claim is even more powerful than 30C, the treating substance is diluted by more than the total number of atoms in the universe. Homeopathy was invented before we knew what atoms were, or how many there are, or how big they are. It has not changed its belief system in light of this information.

How can an almost infinitely dilute solution cure anything? Most homeopaths claim that water has "a memory". They are unclear what this would look like, and homeopaths' experiments claiming to demonstrate it are frequently bizarre. As a brief illustration, American magician and debunker James Randi has for many years had a $1m prize on offer for anyone who can demonstrate paranormal abilities. He has made it clear that this cheque would go to someone who can reliably distinguish a homeopathic dilution from water. His money remains unclaimed.

Many homeopaths also claim they can transmit homeopathic remedies over the internet, in CDs, down the telephone, through a computer, or in a piece of music. Peter Chappell, whose work will feature at a conference organised by the Society of Homeopaths next month, makes dramatic claims about his ability to solve the Aids epidemic using his own homeopathic pills called "PC Aids", and his specially encoded music. "Right now," he says, "Aids in Africa could be significantly ameliorated by a simple tune played on the radio."

EVALUATING THE AUTHOR'S ARGUMENTS:

Goldacre says homeopathic remedies are ineffective. After reading his viewpoint, what do you think is Goldacre's primary reason for drawing this conclusion? Support your answer.

Chiropractic Is Effective

National Center for Complementary and Alternative Medicine

"Chiropractic was one of the 10 most commonly used CAM therapies."

In the following viewpoint the National Center for Complementary and Alternative Medicine (NCCAM) introduces chiropractic care as a legitimate practice, with a foundation in self-healing. NCCAM reports that about 20 percent of American adults have received chiropractic care at some point, and 53 percent of those Americans found combining chiropractic services with conventional medical treatments was effective. NCCAM also funds research in support of chiropractic care. The National Center for Complementary and Alternative Medicine is the federal government's lead agency for scientific research on complementary and alternative medicine (CAM).

AS YOU READ, CONSIDER THE FOLLOWING QUESTIONS:
1. What are some reasons that people seek chiropractic care?
2. Where does the word "chiropractic" come from? How does this relate to the actual practice?
3. NCCAM suggests that chiropractic patients about to receive care must give the chiropractor a "full picture" of what they do to manage their health. Considering the background of chiropractic care, how would the "full picture" ensure an effective treatment?

National Center for Complementary and Alternative Medicine, "An Introduction to Chiropractic," *Backgrounder,* November 2007. Reproduced by permission of www.nccam.nih.gov.

Chiropractic is a health care approach that focuses on the relationship between the body's structure—mainly the spine—and its functioning. Although practitioners may use a variety of treatment approaches, they primarily perform adjustments to the spine or other parts of the body with the goal of correcting alignment problems and supporting the body's natural ability to heal itself.

Key Points About Chiropractic

- People seek chiropractic care primarily for pain conditions such as back pain, neck pain, and headache.
- Side effects and risks depend on the type of chiropractic treatment used.
- Chiropractic practitioners in the United States are required to earn a Doctor of Chiropractic degree from properly accredited colleges.
- Ongoing research is looking at effects of chiropractic treatment approaches, how they might work, and diseases and conditions for which they may be most helpful.
- Tell your health care providers about any complementary and alternative practices you use. Give them a full picture of what you do to manage your health. This will help ensure coordinated and safe care.

The term "chiropractic" combines the Greek words *cheir* (hand) and *praxis* (action) to describe a treatment done by hand. Hands-on therapy—especially adjustment of the spine—is central to chiropractic care. Chiropractic . . . is considered part of complementary and alternative medicine (CAM). [CAM is a group of diverse medical and health care systems, practices, and products that are not presently considered to be part of conventional medicine. Complementary medicine is used together with conventional medicine, and alternative medicine is used in place of conventional medicine.] CAM is based on these key concepts:

- The body has a powerful self-healing ability.
- The body's structure (primarily that of the spine) and its function are closely related, and this relationship affects health.
- Therapy aims to normalize this relationship between structure and function and assist the body as it heals.

While some procedures associated with chiropractic care can be traced back to ancient times, the modern profession of chiropractic was founded by Daniel David Palmer in 1895 in Davenport, Iowa. Palmer, a self-taught healer, believed that the body has a natural healing ability. Misalignments of the spine can interfere with the flow of energy needed to support health, Palmer theorized, and the key to health is to normalize the function of the nervous system, especially the spinal cord.

A chiropractor treats a woman's back. Treatment of the nervous system through spinal subsystems allows the body to increase its inherent ability to self-heal, proponents say.

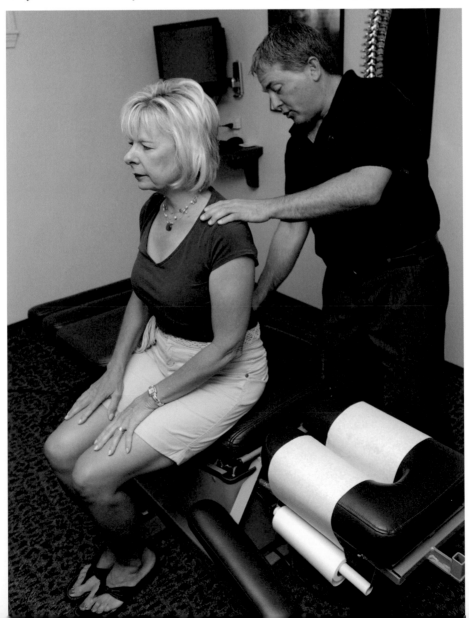

Patterns of Use

A 2002 national survey on CAM use found that about 20 percent of American adults had received chiropractic care at some point during their lives. Chiropractic was one of the 10 most commonly used CAM therapies. Those surveyed reported using chiropractic treatment for the following reasons:

- Combining chiropractic services with conventional medical treatments would help—53 percent
- Conventional medicine would not help—40 percent
- Chiropractic would be interesting to try—32 percent
- Conventional medical professional suggested it—20 percent
- Conventional medical treatments were too expensive—10 percent.

Many people who seek chiropractic care have chronic, pain-related health conditions. Low-back pain, neck pain, and headache are common conditions for which people seek chiropractic treatment.

What to Expect from Chiropractic Visits

During the initial visit, chiropractors typically take a health history and perform a physical examination, with a special emphasis on the spine. Other examinations or tests such as x-rays may also be performed. If chiropractic treatment is considered appropriate, a treatment plan will be developed.

> **FAST FACT**
>
> In 1951 Mutual of Omaha became the first private insurance company to cover chiropractic services.

During followup visits, practitioners may perform one or more of the many different types of adjustments used in chiropractic care. Given mainly to the spine, a chiropractic adjustment (sometimes referred to as a manipulation) involves using the hands or a device to apply a controlled, sudden force to a joint, moving it beyond its passive range of motion. The goal is to increase the range and quality of motion in the area being treated and to aid in restoring health. Other hands-on therapies such as mobilization (movement of a joint within its usual range of motion) also may be used.

Chiropractors may combine the use of spinal adjustments with several other treatments and approaches such as:

- Heat and ice
- Electrical stimulation
- Rest
- Rehabilitative exercise
- Counseling about diet, weight loss, and other lifestyle factors
- Dietary supplements.

Side Effects and Risks

Side effects and risks depend on the specific type of chiropractic treatment used. For example, side effects from chiropractic adjustments can include temporary headaches, tiredness, or discomfort in parts of the body that were treated. The likelihood of serious complications, such as stroke, appears to be extremely low and related to the type of adjustment performed and the part of the body treated.

If dietary supplements are a part of the chiropractic treatment plan, they may interact with medicines and cause side effects. It is important that people inform their chiropractors of all medicines (whether prescription or over-the-counter) and supplements they are taking.

Qualifications for Chiropractors to Practice

To practice chiropractic care in the United States, a practitioner must earn a Doctor of Chiropractic (D.C.) degree from a college accredited by the Council on Chiropractic Education (CCE). CCE is the agency certified by the U.S. Department of Education to accredit chiropractic colleges in the United States. Admission to a chiropractic college requires a minimum of 90 semester hour credits (approximately 3 years) of undergraduate study, mostly in the sciences.

Chiropractic training is a 4-year academic program that includes both classroom work and direct experience caring for patients. Coursework typically includes instruction in the biomedical sciences, as well as in public health and research methods. Some chiropractors pursue a 2- to 3-year residency for training in specialized fields.

Other Points to Consider

Research to expand the scientific understanding of chiropractic treatment is ongoing. If you decide to seek chiropractic care, talk to your chiropractor about:

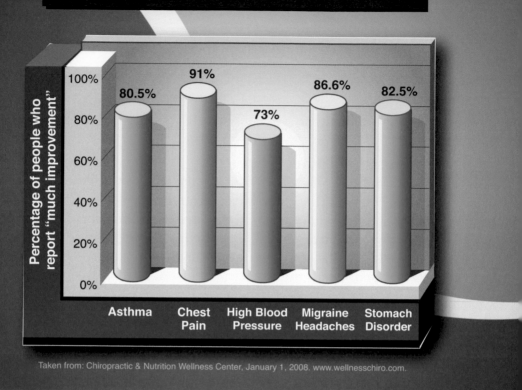

Effectiveness of Chiropractic Treatment

Percentage of people who report "much improvement"

Asthma	80.5%
Chest Pain	91%
High Blood Pressure	73%
Migraine Headaches	86.6%
Stomach Disorder	82.5%

Taken from: Chiropractic & Nutrition Wellness Center, January 1, 2008. www.wellnesschiro.com.

- His education, training, and licensing
- Whether he has experience treating the health conditions for which you are seeking care
- Any special medical concerns you have and any medicines or dietary supplements you are taking.

Tell all of your health care providers about any complementary and alternative practices you use. Give them a full picture of what you do to manage your health. This will help ensure coordinated and safe care.

Recent research projects on chiropractic care supported by the National Center for Complementary and Alternative Medicine (NCCAM) have focused on the:

- Effectiveness of chiropractic treatments for back pain, neck pain, and headache, as well as for other health conditions such as temporomandibular [jaw] disorders

- Development of a curriculum to increase the number of chiropractors involved in research
- Influence of people's satisfaction with chiropractic care on their response to treatment.

Chiropractic Is Mostly Ineffective

Bruce Thyer and Gary Whittenberger

"Skeptics fear that chiropractors ... often ... create expectations that chiropractic can cure or heal medical problems for which it is ill suited."

In the following viewpoint Bruce Thyer and Gary Whittenberger contend that chiropractors are causing harm by making false claims about what conditions they can treat. Thyer and Whittenberger say that chiropractic may be useful in treating back or spinal pain but there is nothing to show that it can treat any other ailment. The authors say that despite this, chiropractors are claiming to treat a wide range of disorders. This sort of inappropriate chiropractic treatment wastes money, prevents people from getting real medical treatment, and can cause serious physical harm to patients, they say. Thyer and Whittenberger are members of a Tallahassee, Florida, skeptics group called the Center for Inquiry.

AS YOU READ, CONSIDER THE FOLLOWING QUESTIONS:

1. According to Thyer and Whittenberger, who was primarily responsible for the establishment of the chiropractic profession in the United States?
2. What percentage of chiropractic offices told Thyer they could treat high blood pressure, arthritis, or both?
3. According to Thyer and Whittenberger, what caused Stephen Barrett to terminate his chiropractic study in the 1970s?

Bruce Thyer and Gary Whittenberger, "A Skeptical Consumer's Look at Chiropractic Claims: Flimflam in Florida?" *Skeptical Inquirer,* January/February 2008. Reproduced by permission.

T he late Carl Sagan said, "Extraordinary claims require extraordinary evidence." This skeptical principle can be applied generally to the area of consumer affairs and more specifically to the claims of chiropractic, an "alternative healing" approach now practiced widely throughout the United States and other parts of the world.

What Is Chiropractic?

Chiropractic practice began in 1895, when D.D. Palmer administered a "chiropractic adjustment" to a deaf man who reportedly regained his hearing. Palmer, a grocer and "magnetic healer", made great claims about the importance of his new treatment for human ailments. According to Palmer, "A subluxated vertebrae . . . is the cause of 95 percent of all diseases . . . the other 5 percent is caused by displaced joints other than those of the vertebral column."

The very existence of vertebral subluxations and their etiological role in health problems is uncertain and subject to considerable controversy, since there is very little empirical evidence in support of the efficacy of chiropractic.

J.J. Palmer, the son of chiropractic's founder, was primarily responsible for the development of chiropractic as a profession within the United States. In a little more than a hundred years, chiropractic has advanced dramatically to the point where there are now sixteen accredited colleges of chiropractic and fifty thousand licensed chiropractors in the U.S. alone.

Within the state of Florida, where the current study was initiated, chiropractic medicine is defined by law as "a noncombative principle and practice consisting of the science of the adjustment, manipulation, and treatment of the human body in which vertebral subluxations and other malpositioned articulations and structures that are interfering with the normal generation, transmission, and expression of nerve impulses between the brain, organs, and tissue cells of the body, thereby causing disease, are adjusted, manipulated, or treated, thus restoring the normal flow of nerve impulse which produces normal function and consequent health. . . ." In 1998, Florida, with its four thousand practitioners, ranked fourth in the nation in the number of licensed chiropractors.

It is generally agreed that chiropractic may be a useful approach in alleviating pain for a very limited set of disorders associated with the

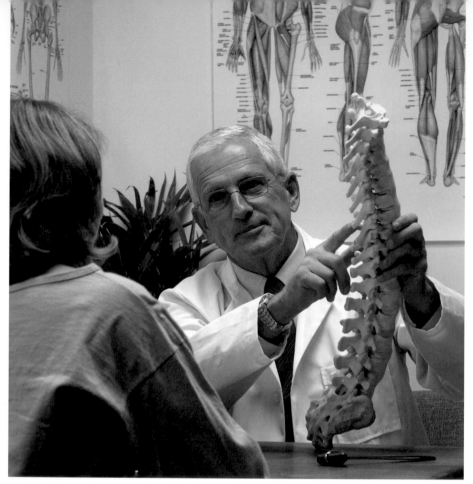

A chiropractor shows a model of the human spine while consulting with a patient. Critics say chiropractics may be useful in treating back pain but little else.

back or spine. However, many skeptics are concerned that chiropractic is being applied to disorders for which it is an inappropriate intervention and for which solid evidence of its efficacy is lacking. If this is the case, then several unfortunate consequences might result. Patients might be harmed by the treatment itself, they might waste their time and money, or they might be deterred from seeking effective treatments. Skeptics fear that chiropractors and their representatives may often promise too much and create expectations that chiropractic can cure or heal medical problems for which it is ill suited.

Are Chiropractors in Tallahassee Treating Inappropriately?

This study was designed to ascertain the degree to which the representatives of chiropractic in a medium-sized Florida city would agree to treat a patient presenting complaints for which chiropractic has not been shown to be effective. The setting for this study was Tallahassee, the capital of Florida, with a population of approximately 151,000 people and where both the authors of this article reside. The local telephone book lists about thirty-three chiropractors in the city. Bruce Thyer contacted the offices of most of these practitioners by telephone during the months of December 2005 and January 2006 and was successful in reaching someone in the office in twenty-eight of the cases. Thyer used a standard opening script for each call: "Good afternoon, my name is Bruce and I am fifty-two. I am interested in learning if chiropractic can help me with high blood pressure and arthritis." Occasionally, after an initial response, Thyer would ask for confirmation by saying "So you treat people with high blood pressure and arthritis?" In nearly every case, the call was received by a secretary, receptionist, technician, or someone representing the chiropractor, not by the chiropractor himself. So, how often did the representatives of chiropractors agree to treat a fifty-two-year-old man with high blood pressure and arthritis?

Most Responses Are Positive
Twenty-one of the twenty-eight offices (75 percent) said that they could treat high blood pressure, arthritis, or both; two of the twenty-eight (7 percent) said they did not treat either of the disorders; and three of the twenty-eight (11 percent) indicated that they didn't know or were uncertain if these problems could be treated.

Among the positive responses were the following:
- "Absolutely, all the time."
- "Yes, definitely."
- "Yes, it should help."
- "Yes it can."
- "It has been known to be of great benefit for both."
- "I know it will help with the high blood pressure, and with the arthritis it will help maintain you, but it will not cure you."
- "Not high blood pressure, but arthritis, yes."
- "Yeah, sometimes, especially the high blood pressure part."

- "The arthritis . . . and generally, yes, blood pressure. He can help you in terms of making you feel better."
- "Sure, I can administer the adjustments, open up the joints and improve blood flow."
- "Can probably help with the pain of arthritis, but blood pressure, no that would need to get homeopathy treatment and he does that too."
- "Yes, the doctor can treat that [high blood pressure and arthritis]. What insurance do you have?"

Negative responses included:

- "Generally that is not what chiropractic does."
- "Primarily [we] focus on spinal and orthopedic problems, not arthritis or high blood pressure."

Uncertain responses included:

- "This is something we would need to talk to the doctor about, and he is out of town."

In the end, three-quarters of the representatives of chiropractors in Tallahassee agreed that their offices would be able to treat someone with high blood pressure and/or arthritis. Now, it might be argued that the chiropractors themselves would have given responses much different from those obtained in this study. Maybe they would not have been as agreeable to the treatment of high blood pressure and arthritis as their employees were. At worst, the office employees were accurately representing the intentions of the chiropractors for which they work, and those chiropractors were offering treatment for high blood pressure and arthritis. At best, the employees were misrepresenting the intentions of the chiropractors for which they work and were promising too much, in which case the employees were not properly trained to interact with prospective patients. Neither outcome is in the best interest of the public.

Similar Results in Ontario, Canada
Results similar to those of this study have been reported elsewhere. Recently, a reporter in Ontario, Canada, posed as a mother seeking

treatment for her two-year-old son's chronic ear infections. She called the offices of fifty randomly selected chiropractors and asked if the chiropractors provided treatment for young children and if they would be able to help with a child's ear infections. Forty-five of the fifty offices (80 percent) said they treated young children and thirty-six of the fifty (72 percent) said they could help with the ear infections. These expectations were given even though the glosso-pharyngeal nerve in the ear doesn't go through the spine, which is the intended target of chiropractic.

In the 1970s, physician Stephen Barrett supervised a woman who took her healthy four-year-old daughter to five chiropractors for a "checkup." Prior to these visits, the child was examined by a pediatrician and found to be healthy. The mother carried a concealed tape recorder during the visits. One chiropractor ran a "nervoscope" up and down the child's spine for a minute and said she had pinched nerves to the stomach and gallbladder, and he recommended X-rays. The second chiropractor said the child's pelvis was twisted and needed adjusting. The third found one hip to be elevated, and recommended adjustments. The fourth found a shorter leg and neck tension, and recommended weekly adjustments. And the fifth found hip and neck misalignments and without permission provided adjustments to the four-year-old. The screams of the child during the adjustments, heard over the tape recorder, caused Dr. Barrett to terminate this study. Later, as an eleven-year-old, the girl was in good health and a gymnast.

The Costs of Inappropriate Chiropractic Treatment

There is evidence from this study and other similar investigations that chiropractors or their representatives are agreeing to treat, and possibly attempting to treat, disorders for which their practice is not appropriate. In a sense, they are advertising that they can effectively treat certain disorders when there are few or no controlled clinical

Chiropractic Claims

The following is a list of conditions that chiropractors say may indicate you have a spinal subluxation, or misalignment.

Allergies	Arm Pain/Numbness
Arthritis	Asthma
Attention Deficit Disorder	Auto Injuries
Back Pain	Bedwetting
Blood Pressure Problems	Bursitis
Carpal Tunnel Syndrome	Digestive Disorders
Disc Problems	Dizziness
Epilepsy	Fatigue/Lack of Energy
Female Disorders	Foot Pain
Frequent Colds	Frequent Ear Infections
Hand and Wrist Pain	Hip Pain
Joint Pains	Knee Pain
Leg Pain/Numbness	Lifting Injuries
Lowered Resistance	Migraine Headaches
Neck Pain/Stiffness	Nervousness
Pinched Nerve	Poor Circulation
Premenstrual Syndrome	Sciatica
Shingles	Shoulder Pain
Sinusitis	Spinal Curvatures
Spinal Injuries	Stiffness
Stomach Ulcers	Stress/Tension Headaches
Tingling and Numbness	Turned-in Feet
Whiplash Injuries	Work Injuries

Taken from: Stephen Barrett, "Conditions That May Indicate You Have a Spinal Subluxation."
www.chirobase.org, June 21, 2006.

studies that actually back up these claims. Thus, many of the claims of chiropractic can be considered extraordinary, and as Sagan would remind us, these claims require extraordinary evidence before they should be believed.

We also suggest that the approach used in this study, calling up health care providers and asking them about the types of disorders they claim to treat, is a very useful and low-cost investigative strategy that can be adopted by skeptical consumers in their local communities. Our study revealed that the large majority of chiropractic offices contacted claimed to be able to treat hypertension and arthritis, claims that the current scientific literature does not justify. The costs to consumers who are seeking legitimate and effective treatments for these serious health problems, and who instead receive inappropriate and ineffective diagnostic (e.g., spinal radiographs) and therapeutic procedures (spinal manipulation), are undoubtedly substantial. So, too, are the costs to private, state, and federal health insurance providers. The extent to which consumers are diverted from receiving evidence-based treatments for serious health problems is similarly unknown but also likely to be considerable.

EVALUATING THE AUTHORS' ARGUMENTS:

Bruce Thyer and Gary Whittenberger are members of a skeptics group. Skeptics are naturally disbelieving of extraordinary claims unless there is substantial scientific evidence. Do you think chiropractors' claims are extraordinary? Did Thyer and Whittenberger provide enough evidence to convince you of their disbelief? Why or why not?

Chapter 2

Does Alternative Medicine Help Fight Disease?

Alternative medicine treatments for cancer include curcumin, which is derived from the herb turmeric.

Alternative Medicine Can Cure Cancer

R. Webster Kehr

"What you know about cancer has been carefully designed and crafted by the pharmaceutical industry propaganda artists to keep you in the dark about the vast superiority of Mother Nature at treating cancer."

In the following viewpoint R. Webster Kehr argues that alternative medicine can cure cancer, but the public is largely unaware of this fact because they have been brainwashed to believe that cancer can be treated only with chemotherapy, radiation, or surgery. Kehr believes that most mainstream medical doctors are in cahoots with the pharmaceutical industry to suppress the use of cancer-stopping alternative medicine because they cannot make money from natural molecules. The medical establishment is completely happy to *slow* cancer using expensive and harmful methods, says Kehr, because this way they make billions of dollars. Kehr maintains an alternative medicine cancer treatment Web site (http://cancertutor. com). This viewpoint was taken from Kehr's foreword to the book *Cancer: Step Outside the Box*, which was written by Ty Bollinger.

AS YOU READ, CONSIDER THE FOLLOWING QUESTIONS:
1. Cancer cells are described as being "undifferentiated." What does this mean, according to Kehr?
2. According to the author, what would happen to patients who took enough chemotherapy drugs to kill all of their cancer cells?
3. What is orthodox medicine's true cure rate over cancer, according to Kehr?

One day I came home from work and my wife happened to be in one of the bedrooms. I walked into the bedroom and she looked at me and said: "*I went to the doctor today and he said I have diabetes.*" As near as I can remember, these are the exact words I said to her: "*So what? The cure for type 2 diabetes is on my website, just go to my website.*" I then walked out of the room without another word being spoken. A couple of hours later I concluded I had been a bit brash, so I went to the health food store and bought the things she needed that I could buy locally, then I ordered the rest from the Internet. Within 2 months she was able to quit monitoring her blood glucose. . . .

Had my wife told me her doctor told her she had breast cancer or pancreatic cancer or just about any other kind of cancer, my response to her would have been identical, except for substituting whatever kind of cancer she had for the term "*type 2 diabetes.*". . . Curing newly diagnosed cancer is easy; however, there are a few kinds of cancer (*like squamous cell carcinoma*) for which you need to pick the correct treatment the first time or you may not get a second chance.

A Cancer Cell Is Useless

A cancer cell is described as being "undifferentiated." What this means is that a cancer cell has no useful function. For example, a group of cancer cells cannot form muscle tissue, nor can a cancer cell become a functional part of muscle tissue. A cancer cell cannot become a functional part of a heart muscle. It cannot perform a function as part of the liver. A cancer cell can do nothing that is constructive. It just sits there. A cancer cell is like a blob of oil—you cannot integrate it into the frame of an automobile while it is still a blob of oil.

In a similar way a cancer cell cannot become part of tumor tissue, since tumor tissue must be composed entirely of healthy cells. The cancer cells just sit inside the tumor tissue, doing nothing except multiplying and refusing to die. Biopsies essentially are looking for cancer cells that are just sitting there. Because the majority of the cells in a tumor are healthy cells (*all of the functional cells are healthy cells*), there are not enough cancer cells inside a tumor to kill a person. In other words, no person has ever died from the cancer cells inside a tumor. This is because there cannot be enough cancer cells in a tumor to kill a person. Likewise, no one ever died from the cancer cells inside of the prostate gland. Benign tumors have grown to hundreds of pounds and still not killed the patient.

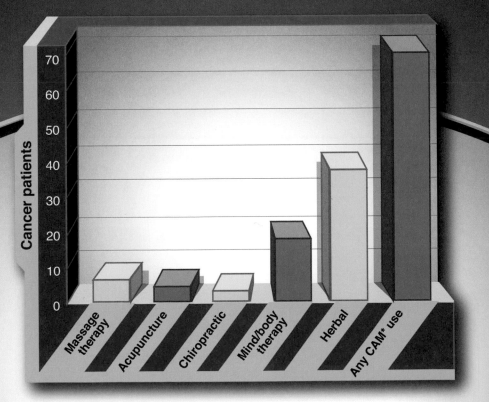

Complementary and Alternative Medicine Use in Cancer Patients

* Complementary and Alternative Medicine

Taken from: William Lafferty et al., Center for Palliative Care Education, University of Washington, 2003.

Spreading Cancer Cells Matter

What kills cancer patients is the *spreading* of their cancer cells. When the cancer spreads enough, there are enough cancer cells to kill a person. A large number of cancer cells will literally suck the life out of a cancer patient by stealing glucose and nutrients from healthy cells by creating toxins like lactic acid. But in order to kill a person, the spreading has to go far beyond any tumor (*there are rare exceptions to this rule, such as when a tumor is blocking the flow of vital fluids*). Yet, in spite of these facts, oncologists continue to talk to patients about their tumors.

This quote, by the late Dr. Philip Binzel, M.D., explains what I am talking about.

> When a patient is found to have a tumor, the only thing the doctor discusses with that patient is what he intends to do about the tumor. If a patient with a tumor is receiving radiation or chemotherapy, the only question that is asked is, "How is the tumor doing?" No one ever asks how the patient is doing. In my medical training, I remember well seeing patients who were getting radiation and/or chemotherapy. The tumor would get smaller and smaller, but the patient would be getting sicker and sicker. At autopsy we would hear, "Isn't that marvelous! The tumor is gone!" Yes, it was, but so was the patient. *How many millions of times are we going to have to repeat these scenarios before we realize that we are treating the wrong thing?*
>
> In primary cancer, with only a few exceptions, the tumor is neither health-endangering nor life-threatening. I am going to repeat that statement. In primary cancer, with few exceptions, the tumor is neither health-endangering nor life-threatening. *What is health-endangering and life-threatening is the spread of that disease through the rest of the body.* There is nothing in surgery that will prevent the spread of cancer. There is nothing in radiation that will prevent the spread of the disease. There is nothing in chemotherapy that will prevent the spread of the disease. How do we know? Just look at the statistics! There is a statistic known as "survival time." Survival time is defined as that interval of time between when the diagnosis of cancer is first made in a given patient and when that patient dies from his disease.

In the past fifty years, tremendous progress has been made in the early diagnosis of cancer. In that period of time, tremendous progress had been made in the surgical ability to remove tumors. Tremendous progress has been made in the use of radiation and chemotherapy in their ability to shrink or destroy tumors. *But, the survival time of the cancer patient today is no greater than it was fifty years ago.* What does this mean? It obviously means that we are treating the wrong thing! . . .

In a nutshell, Dr. Binzel is saying is that nothing in orthodox medicine stops the spread of the cancer. You might think that chemotherapy is designed to stop the spread of cancer. Chemotherapy does not target cancer cells. It kills fast growing cells, whether cancerous or non-cancerous. Some cancer cells are not fast growing, thus chemotherapy may not kill them. Some cancer cells develop a resistance to synthetic drugs, so chemotherapy cannot kill them, etc.

Mainstream Medicine Does Not Stop the Spread of Cancer

The bottom line is that if a person took enough chemotherapy to kill all of their cancer cells, the patient would die from the toxicity of chemotherapy long before the cancer cells would all be killed. *Chemotherapy can only slow down the cancer; it cannot stop it from spreading and killing the patient.* Chemotherapy puts people in "remission," but in almost all cases the patient will come out of remission and die. Many cancer patients don't live long enough to go into remission, others go into remission several times.

Surgery certainly does not stop cancer that has already spread because in almost every case the cancer has spread far beyond what a surgeon can cut out. Radiation is like a rifle. Can you put out a carpet fire (i.e. *a spreading cancer*) with a rifle? The only thing orthodox medicine can do is shrink tumors and slow down the cancer and temporarily put patients in remission; orthodox medicine cannot stop the spreading of cancer—*period*!!!

What this means is that the Food and Drug Administration (*FDA*) has *never* approved a chemotherapy drug that can target cancer cells or stop the spread of cancer. Every chemotherapy drug they have ever approved is virtually worthless or does more harm than good.

Furthermore, the American Medical Association (*AMA, which is nothing but a labor union*) has *never* approved a procedure that can stop the spread of cancer.

They Want to Slow, Not Stop, Cancer

No medical doctor . . . has ever administered a synthetic drug or done a medical procedure that stopped the spread of cancer. That is not what they do. What they do is slow down the cancer, in some cases. You might ask: do they want to stop the spread of cancer and cure the patient? While individual doctors may want to cure their patients, as far as an industry is concerned, the evidence is overwhelming that the answer to that question is *"no"*!! . . .

There is a pattern in medicine that effective cancer treatments are shut down from public view and highly *ineffective* synthetic drugs (*they are profitable because they can be patented*) are routinely approved by the FDA. It is a scam the likes of which the world has never before seen. Future doctors will look at this generation of "doctors" in total disgust. They have had many opportunities to cure cancer, but rather than cure cancer, they bury the treatment and make it illegal to use.

The only logical motto to assign to both Big Pharma (*the pharmaceutical industry*) and Big Medicine (*the AMA*) is this: *"It is far, far more profitable to slow down the spread of cancer than to stop the spread of cancer. Everything that stops the spread of cancer must be shut down."*

The long term goal of the quid pro quo marriage made in hell between the FDA, AMA and Big Pharma (i.e. *the core of the "Cancer Industry"*), is to make cancer into a chronic disease like diabetes, whereby the patient becomes a long-term profit center. Just look at the newspapers. Almost every week some new drug is approved by the FDA that extends the life of cancer patients, compared to prior worthless drugs. That is exactly what they want to do. You will never

> ## FAST FACT
>
> A study reported in the July 2000 issue of the *Journal of Clinical Oncology* found that 69 percent of 453 cancer patients had used at least one complementary or alternative therapy as part of their cancer treatment.

see a cure for a cancer unless it is an extremely rare type of cancer; such that the public relations propaganda is of more financial benefit to the Cancer Industry than the money lost to the cure. You will *never* see a cure for breast cancer, for example.

The child of the marriage made in hell is the American Cancer Society propaganda machine that is tasked to make orthodox cancer treatments look far, far more effective than they really are. They are the makeup artists for the monster. You probably think the true cure rate of orthodox medicine is 40% to 50% and growing rapidly. Nope. It has been 3% for the last 80 years and it isn't going anywhere.

Mother Nature Knows About Cancer

Are there any natural cancer treatments (i.e. *alternative cancer treatments*), meaning the use of molecules from Mother Nature, that have been shown to target cancer cells and stop the spread of cancer and cure a patient? You probably think the answer is "no." That would be the wrong answer. There are dozens of alternative cancer treatments that can stop the spread of cancer and even cure the cancer completely. . . .

However, as you might suspect, the FDA has *never* approved one of these cancer treatments because the drug companies have never submitted one of them to the FDA. This is partly because Big Pharma cannot patent natural molecules (*and thus make their obscene profits*), and it is partly because the AMA doesn't want cancer to be cured. The AMA does not allow medical doctors to use effective cancer treatments. Since these treatments have not been submitted to the FDA by the pharmaceutical industry, the FDA labels them as "unproven," no matter how much scientific evidence there is for the treatment.

That is why accountants, housewives, farmers, engineers, etc. are leading the battle against the Cancer Industry. But these people have absolutely zero clout with the media. By the way, the FDA, National Cancer Institute (*NCI*), National Institutes of Health (*NIH*), ad nauseam, are *not* the angels in this equation. They too have sold their souls and know exactly what is going on.

Mother Nature's molecules, as a general rule, *always* target cancer cells or do no harm to normal cells. Thus, Mother Nature's molecules can be used in much, much higher doses than Big Pharma's molecules. That is why Mother Nature has a true cure rate that is

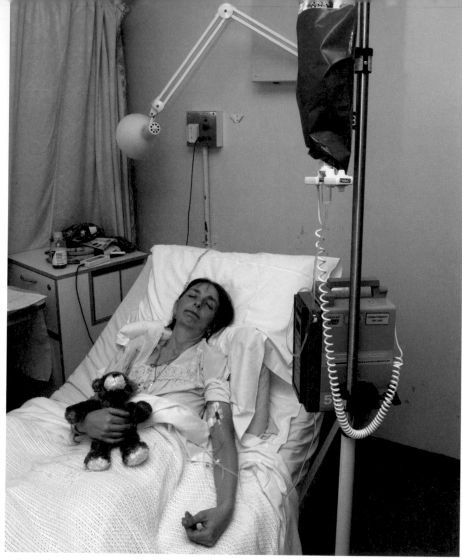

The author argues that chemotherapy can only slow down cancer and cannot stop it from spreading and killing the patient.

thirty times higher than orthodox medicine for recently diagnosed patients!!

Mother Nature (i.e. *God*) knows a lot more about cancer than the pharmaceutical industry chemists. More importantly, Mother Nature has a lot more integrity than the executives of the pharmaceutical companies. Judgment Day will take care of them and their brothers in the tobacco industry, federal government, etc., forever, but that is probably not your immediate concern. Your immediate concern is that Mother Nature knows how to target cancer cells and stop the spreading of cancer.

So why haven't you been brainwashed into believing in alternative medicine? Why haven't you heard these things a thousand times on television or radio or in the major magazines? *Because if they told you these things, the pharmaceutical industry would pull all of their advertising money and give that advertising money to a competing station or magazine.*

Also, to a large degree the same people who make huge profits supplying and working with orthodox medicine also own the large television and radio networks. For example, General Electric, which makes huge profits from supplying hospitals with expensive equipment, and by selling prescription drugs, etc. owns the NBC network and at least 30 major NBC affiliates. General Electric is a member of the Cancer Industry and they own NBC!

Seek Alternative Medicine First

What you know about cancer has been carefully designed and crafted by the pharmaceutical industry propaganda artists to keep you in the dark about the vast superiority of Mother Nature at treating cancer. Unfortunately, some of the people who are on the natural side of the street (i.e. *the alternative medicine people*) do not have any more integrity than the tobacco companies and pharmaceutical companies. . . .

Consider these factual statistics:
- A true cure rate of 90% or more can easily be achieved by cancer patients who avoid orthodox medicine, go with alternative medicine first, and do their homework
- The true cure rate of orthodox medicine is 3% or less
- 95% of cancer patients who go with alternative cancer treatments have previously had the full orthodox treatment and have been sent home to die, meaning alternative medicine is handed a large number of cancer patients already in critical condition
- For those who wait to go with alternative cancer treatments until after they have been sent home to die, only a handful of the 300+ alternative cancer treatments are strong enough to give them a chance of survival
- But even for those rare people who do find one of those potent treatments (e.g. *those who read this book*), at best they only have a chance of survival of about 50%

In other words, if you go with alternative medicine first, *your chance of survival is 90% or more, if you do your homework.* If you go with orthodox medicine first, and then alternative medicine second, you will have years of suffering and if you are lucky you will then have a 50% chance of survival.

EVALUATING THE AUTHOR'S ARGUMENTS:

R. Webster Kehr argues that alternative treatments can cure cancer. He also argues that mainstream medicine wants to slow the spread of cancer rather than cure it. What other arguments can you find in his viewpoint? Do you think he adequately supports his main viewpoint, that alternative medicine can cure cancer? Why or why not?

Alternative Medicine Cannot Cure Cancer

Edzard Ernst

"It is understandable that those who promote alternative medicine at any cost are less than happy with me repeatedly stating that there will never be such a thing as an alternative cancer cure."

In the following viewpoint Edzard Ernst maintains that alternative medicine will never cure cancer. He says cancer drugs must be developed and administered very carefully so they kill only cancer cells and not healthy cells. This is very difficult to do using whole plants or herbs, as most alternative medicine practitioners do. Ernst says that mainstream medicine has been very good at developing cancer drugs, even those that come from plants. He believes the alternative medicine industry may be offering false hope to cancer patients and that this could be endangering their lives. Ernst is a professor of complementary medicine at Peninsula Medical School, Universities of Exeter and Plymouth, and editor in chief of the journal *Focus on Alternative and Complementary Therapies.*

AS YOU READ, CONSIDER THE FOLLOWING QUESTIONS:
1. Ernst says that complementary medicine has a lot to offer cancer patients in therapies used for what?
2. According to the author, what two anticancer drugs come from the common periwinkle plant?
3. According to Ernst, what happened to the two shark species used for commercial preparations of shark cartilage, after shark cartilage was hyped as an alternative cancer cure?

A single Sunday paper can give an impressive insight into how forcefully alternative medicine is currently being promoted. In the *Sunday Times* two months ago (14 August [2005]), it was reported that The Prince of Wales's Foundation for Integrated Health is campaigning to sign up 150 GPs [general practitioners] . . . to become associates. Subsequently, these doctors are "expected to offer a wide range of herbal and other alternative treatments to their patients." In the same issue, health writer Susan Clark advised a reader to use marigold ointment to treat "little cancers that are the result of sun damage to the skin."

It is understandable that those who promote alternative medicine at any cost are less than happy with me repeatedly stating that there will never be such a thing as an alternative cancer cure. They think that I am factually wrong or at least unacceptably negative—after all, as professor of complementary medicine, I should join them in their promotion.

It is important to understand what alternative cancer cures claim to be. They are treatments that change the natural history of the disease by somehow affecting cancer growth. They are, therefore, entirely different from therapies used for palliative care or cancer prevention, for both of which complementary medicine has a lot offer.

Mainstream Versus Alternative Medicine

Plants have given us powerful cancer drugs: the common periwinkle, for instance, fathered [the cancer drugs] vinblastine and vincristine. So why should there not be other such treasures in the plant kingdom? I am sure there are, but they will not become alternative cancer cures—they will, just like these vinca alkaloids or paclitaxel (from the yew tree), most certainly become mainstream treatments.

Some argue that until science discovers and develops such drugs, their natural precursors could still be used by alternative practitioners to cure cancer patients. I do not think so. Before vincristine was developed, herbalists did not prescribe extract of periwinkle for their cancer patients. The plant is highly toxic and would probably have killed more patients than it cured. The active compounds had to be isolated and dosed carefully to threaten only the cancer cells and not the patient.

There are hundreds, if not thousands, of alleged alternative cancer cures. Type "alternative medicine" into Google and you will find over 21 million pages offering information about this topic. Assessing the first 32 sites resulted in an amazing array of alternative cancer cures being recommended. The temptation for desperate cancer patients to try these options must be huge. Yet, I fear, none of them will realise the dream of an alternative cancer cure.

Take shark cartilage, for instance. Based on the (incorrect) notion that sharks do not get cancer, it was promoted as an alternative cancer cure. Amazingly, *in vitro* tests demonstrated that shark cartilage has anti-angiogenic [anti-growth] activity. Such findings made the sales figures rocket and the two shark species used for commercial preparations were driven to the brink of extinction. Finally, the first controlled clinical trial of shark cartilage recently showed that our hopes were in vain: it is no cure after all.

I think this is most illuminating. It indicates that regular scientists and conventional oncologists [cancer doctors] are more than keen to find new anti-cancer drugs. So, if anything looks in the slightest bit promising, they will investigate it. And they do not care whether the potential drug comes from nature or from the laboratory. If the tests turn out to be positive, the result will be a conventional drug—not an alternative cancer cure. Perhaps we will one day see the advent of

> # FAST FACT
> Americans spent an estimated $72.1 billion for cancer treatment in 2004, just under 5 percent of U.S. spending for all medical treatment.

The common periwinkle flower is used to produce the cancer-fighting agents vinblastine and vincristine.

an anti-angiogenic drug modelled on a compound of shark cartilage. If so, it will be to the credit of those who developed it and not to those who earned millions by grinding up shark fins and selling it as an alternative cancer cure.

Paranoia About Big Pharma

All this seems pure common sense. Yet a strange sort of paranoia persists in the realm of alternative medicine. Many believe that mainstream oncology or "big pharma" actively suppresses the fact that shark cartilage or laetrile [derived from apricot pits and used as a possible cancer cure] or the Gerson diet [nutrition-based therapy] or Essiac [a tea believed to treat cancer] etc, could save thousands of lives of severely affected cancer patients. The myth of alternative cancer cures is created and endlessly perpetuated. In the final analysis, it assumes that scientists are without the slightest bit of conscience. This insults those who dedicate their lives to making progress in cancer care. It is also factually incorrect as evidenced over and over again by true developments, such as those mentioned above.

And what about me? Am I really negative when I write about alternative cancer cures? Should I not join the promoters of the uncritical integration of alternative medicine into the NHS [National Health Service of the UK]? If my allegiance were with the manufacturers of alternative medicines or the professional organisations of alternative practitioners, I would certainly be misguided, but it is with the patient or consumer. As my goal is to contribute through rigorous research to the health care of tomorrow, my caution is, I think, well-justified. My alleged negative attitude then becomes an undeniably positive stance. Informing cancer patients that shark cartilage, laetrile, Gerson diet, Essiac and so forth, will do them no good could save lives.

EVALUATING THE AUTHORS' ARGUMENTS:

Edzard Ernst is a professor of complementary medicine. What impact do you think this has on the credibility of his belief that alternative medicine will never cure cancer? Explain. Ernst implies that the reason alternative medicine is promoted is because of money, while R. Webster Kehr, the author of the previous viewpoint, argues that the reason alternative medicine is suppressed is because of money. Whom do you agree with and why?

Alternative Medicine Can Help Fight Autism

Kenneth A. Bock

"The good news . . . is that these 4-A disorders can be remediated and reversed. Children and their families can be healed."

In the following viewpoint Kenneth A. Bock contends that alternative medicine treatments can heal autism, a mental disorder that appears in infancy and/or early childhood. Autistic individuals have problems with communication, language, social bonding, and imagination. Typically, they do not establish close relationships with others and prefer to remain in their own mental worlds. Bock believes American children are in the midst of an epidemic of autism, as well as epidemics of attention deficit hyperactivity disorder (ADHD), asthma, and allergies. He calls these the "4-A Disorders," and he believes they are caused by heavy metals and other environmental toxins. Bock says children with autism need to eliminate toxins from their body using chelation and other therapies. They also need to go on special diets and take nutritional supplements and medications. If they do all these things, Bock believes they can be cured of autism.

Bock is a medical doctor specializing in autism and ADHD. He has authored several books and medical articles on the 4-A disorders.

AS YOU READ, CONSIDER THE FOLLOWING QUESTIONS:
1. According to Bock, what two heavy metals are implicated in the 4-A disorders?
2. What two gastrointestinal disorders, which Bock says are caused by inflammation, are common in autistic children?
3. Name three types of diets that Bock says 4-A children may require or respond favorably to.

In the world's industrialized, developed nations, epidemics of malnutrition, as well as the common childhood infectious illnesses, are almost a thing of the past, due primarily to the technological advances of our industrial era. However, we are in the midst of a group of new childhood epidemics, which are directly related to this same industrialism and to its associated pollution, environmental degradation, and toxicity. One set of epidemics has, unfortunately, been replaced by another.

I have termed the new childhood epidemics "The 4-A Disorders." They include autism, ADHD, asthma and allergies. Over the past two decades, autism has increased 1500%, while ADHD, asthma and allergies have increased, by some estimates, as much as 300–400%. These are staggering statistics, and these meteoric increases demand explanations.

This concomitant rise is not coincidence. All of these disorders appear to be tied together by a similar mechanism: an underlying genetic vulnerability, triggered by environmental insults. The primary underlying genetic vulnerability appears to be, in many children, an impaired ability to detoxify, which has left them unable to cope with the increasing toxicity to which they are exposed. These toxins include numerous chemicals and heavy metals. Many of these chemicals and heavy metals are neurotoxic, as well as toxic to the immune system. . . .

Heavy Metals and Toxic Chemicals

Heavy metals implicated in the 4-A disorders include mercury and lead. The effects of low-dose mercury toxicity on various organ systems include: deficits in language, memory, and attention; disruption of fine motor function; atopic eczema; and immune dysregulation, including immune deficiency, and autoimmunity. This constellation of damage often results in a diagnosis of autism, ADHD, asthma, or allergy. . . .

Recent research has also shown that low levels of lead, even below the current designated level of concern . . ., can be harmful to the developing brains and nervous systems of fetuses and young children. These small amounts of lead may contribute to behavioral problems, learning disabilities, and/or lower intelligence scores in children.

In addition, biological insults from both lead and mercury, as well as some chemicals, can lead to a Th2 (T helper type 2)-skewed immune system, with an increase in humoral or antibody immunity, as compared to cellular immunity. This can result in excessive allergies and autoimmunity. . . .

Inflammation Should Be Monitored

Chronic inflammation is another primary causative factor that appears to underlie these new childhood epidemics. This inflammation occurs via a cascade of biological processes. First, impaired detoxification leads to an overload of toxins in the body, and these excess toxins can then lead to oxidative stress, and to chronic inflammatory conditions. In autism and asthma, there is ample evidence of increased oxidative stress and chronic inflammation, and there is also chronic inflammation present in chronic allergic states. In addition, ADHD has been associated with chronic allergies.

We often see this inflammation in multiple organ systems, including the gastrointestinal systems of many children with autism, who often suffer particularly from esophagitis and colitis. Many children, in addition to their asthma and neurodevelopmental disorders, also have atopic eczema. . . .

The key to resolving inflammation, in an integrative approach, is to always look for what's driving the inflammation. The driving force may be underlying infections, or it may be allergies or sensitivities to foods and inhalants, or it may be exposure to toxic heavy metals and chemicals. These factors, often in combinations, may underlie and contribute to chronic inflammation. Therefore, they must be eliminated, or at least decreased. . . .

A child who has a 4-A disorder drinks a supplement of antioxidant vitamins as part of his ongoing autism therapy.

In addition, many of the 4-A children, when viewed from a biomedical perspective, have multiple nutritional defiencies and imbalances, as well as metabolic imbalances, and all of these conditions must be addressed, in order to resolve the underlying chronic inflammation. We must also remediate immunological imbalances, including Th2 skewing and lack of adequate immunoregulation.

To effectively overcome the inflammation, oxidative stress, nutritional deficiencies, immune dysfunction, and the other disparate factors that often result in a diagnosis of one of the 4-A disorders, a comprehensive treatment program must be initiated. This program consists of five primary elements: decreasing environmental exposures, dietary modification, nutritional supplementation, detoxification, and administration of medication.

Five Elements to Combat the 4-A Disorders

Decreasing environmental exposures is crucial to stopping this chronic inflammatory process. Exposure to a variety of toxins, including arsenic in chicken; mercury in large fish; lead in soil, water or dust;

pesticides in various foods; and numerous types of polybrominated compounds must be reduced and eliminated if possible in order to allow the process of healing to begin. Additionally, avoiding allergens and treating underlying infections, which can frequently be covert, are keys to helping the body recover from chronic ongoing inflammation and oxidative stress.

Dietary modification is almost always pivotally important. Most 4-A children suffer from significant nutritional deficiencies, which not only contribute to neurological dysfunction, but also to other metabolic processes that disrupt the proper functions of the body and brain. Also, most 4-A children have food allergies and sensitivities that harm the way that they think and feel. Many other 4-A children suffer from other neurologically disruptive conditions that are related to diet, such as hypoglycemia, carbohydrate intolerance, and intestinal hyperpermeability. These children often respond positively to a gluten-free/casein free-diet, avoiding food allergens, and at times, an anti-yeast diet and/or anti-hypoglycemia diet. Some children may require further dietary modifications, including the specific carbohydrate diet (SCD), or occasionally, the low oxalate diet (LOD).

Nutritional supplementation is virtually always needed to support healing. Because there is a significant overlap in the causative factors of the 4-A disorders, there is also often a significant overlap in the nutritional supplement programs that benefit the children suffering from these new childhood epidemics. For example, many of these children, regardless of their discrete diagnoses, benefit from the minerals magnesium, zinc, selenium, chromium and iron, the latter of which can enhance attention, cognition and energy. 4-A children also typically respond to antioxidant vitamins, including, A, C and E, as well as the B vitamins B-6 and methylcobalamin.

FAST FACT

According to a survey by the Autism Research Institute, 76 percent of parents whose children underwent chelation therapy reported that their children "got better."

Other widely effective nutrients include targeted amino acids and anti-inflammatory essential fatty acids, such as EPA [eicosapentaenoic

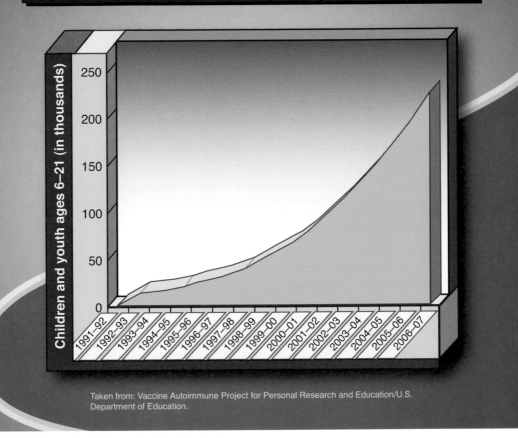

Number of Children with Autism in U.S. Schools

Children and youth ages 6–21 (in thousands)

Taken from: Vaccine Autoimmune Project for Personal Research and Education/U.S. Department of Education.

acid] and DHA [docosahexanoic acid], which are found in fish oils, and gamma linolenic acid (GLA).

Probiotics are also markedly helpful for restoring proper microbial balance in the gastrointestinal system, and for helping to balance Th2-skewing of the immune system, as well as to enhance immunoregulation. More and more research is emerging that supports the therapeutic role of probiotics in allergies, as well as the related conditions of asthma, autism and ADHD.

Detoxification, the essential process of eliminating toxins from the body, can be significantly improved in many children, particularly those who suffer from impaired detoxification abilities. One method for improving detoxification is to administer nutritional and herbal substances, such as glutathione, methylcobalamin, N-acetyl cysteine, garlic, and thiamine tetrahydrofurfuryldisulfide (TTFD).

Detoxification can also be assisted by the careful use of pharmaceutical chelators, such as DMSA [dimercaptosuccinic acid], and CaEDTA [calcium-ethylenediaminetetraacetic acid]. . . .

Medication, the fifth and final element of the program, is an integral part of treatment for most of the children who suffer from these disorders. Medications can be useful when they are applied early in treatment, to help control behaviors, as the comprehensive program gradually begins to take hold. Medications are also helpful in the mid to latter stages of treatment. They can, for example, help to control inflammation. . . .

In all of the 4-A disorders, a wide variety of medications may be of value, depending upon the individual needs of the child. These medications include anti-infective medications, such as antivirals, antibacterials, antiparasitics and especially antifungals. In addition, some children may benefit from immunomodulatory medications, such as low-dose Naltrexone and intravenous gamma globulin.

Autism and Other 4-A Disorders Can Be Healed

This comprehensive program, when applied cautiously, patiently and systematically, drawing from scientific research and coupled with clinical experience, has been shown to trigger recoveries in children with each of the 4-A disorders. It appears as if this approach may represent one of the most promising avenues of treatment for autism, ADHD, asthma, and allergies.

Nonetheless, the inescapable bad news is that we are now without doubt in the midst of a tragic onslaught of the new childhood epidemics. Our children are growing up in a toxic world, and those who have an impaired ability to detoxify appear to be the proverbial "yellow canaries," who are most affected by these disorders.

The good news, however, is that these 4-A disorders can be remediated and reversed. Children and their families can be healed.

Healing the environment, and decreasing toxic exposures, may ultimately be even more effective than medical treatment at stopping the proliferation of these new childhood epidemics. That task, though, will take time, and will require the cooperation of both government and corporate officials in addition to the efforts of clinicians, researchers, and parents.

For now, our focus must be on healing our children, one at a time. Our grave responsibility, as physicians and as parents, is to allow our children—born of love, and nurtured by those who love them most—to have the healthy, happy lives that all children deserve to have.

EVALUATING THE AUTHOR'S ARGUMENTS:

Kenneth A. Bock contends that children with autism who follow special alternative treatment regimes can be cured of their autism. However, Bock does not use the term "alternative medicine." Why do you think Bock's treatment plan is an example of alternative medicine?

Alternative Medicine Treatments for Autism Are Ineffective

Jeff Grabmeier

"There's no cure for autism, and many parents are willing to believe anything if they come to think it could help their child."

The following viewpoint, written by Jeff Grabmeier of the Ohio State University (OSU) Office of Research Communications, provides information on a symposium called "Outrageous Developmental Disabilities Treatments," which was led by OSU professor James Mulick. According to Mulick, there has been a large increase in the number of fad treatments being promoted to cure autism. Mulick says autism is a developmental disability for which there is no cure. Fad treatments such as chelation therapy, special diets, or nutritional supplements have not proved to be effective for autism and can even be dangerous. The only treatment found to help autism so far is an expensive behavioral treatment consisting of several years of daily sessions where autistic children learn to imitate their teachers. Mulick says it is understandable that parents will try anything to help their autistic children. However, alternative fad treatments may be unsafe and offer false hope. Mulick is a professor in the Department of Pediatrics at the Ohio State University College of Medicine. He is also the editor of a book on fad autism treatments called *Controversial Therapies of Developmental Disabilities: Fad, Fashion, and Science in Professional Practice.*

AS YOU READ, CONSIDER THE FOLLOWING QUESTIONS:
1. What proportion of children was said to have autism when Mulick began treating the disability in the 1970s?
2. According to the author, which fad treatment led to the death of an autistic boy?
3. What is the name of the treatment that Mulick says is the only therapy shown to have a long-term positive effect on autism?

Ineffective or even dangerous fad treatments for autism, always a problem, seem to be growing more pervasive, according to researchers who studied the problem.

"Developmental disabilities like autism are a magnet for all kinds of unsupported or disproved therapies, and it has gotten worse as more children have been diagnosed with autism," said James Mulick, professor of pediatrics and psychology at Ohio State University.

"There's no cure for autism, and many parents are willing to believe anything if they come to think it could help their child."

Outrageous Treatments

Mulick chaired a symposium on "Outrageous Developmental Disabilities Treatments" Aug. 20 [2007] in San Francisco at the annual meeting of the American Psychological Association. The symposium included presentations by several of Mulick's students at Ohio State who participated in a graduate seminar on fad treatments in autism.

Tracy Kettering, a doctoral student in special education at Ohio State, said a Google search for the phrase "autism treatment" yields more than 2.2 million matches.

"You get hundreds of different types of therapies that come up, and many have quotes from parents that claim a particular therapy 'cured' their child," Kettering said.

"It's no wonder that parents want to believe. But very few of these treatments have any evidence to support them."

The number and range of fad treatments has seemed to grow in recent years as more children have been diagnosed with autism, said Mulick. . . .

Mulick said when he began treating autism in the 1970s about 3 children in 10,000 were said to have autism. Now, reports are 1 in 166 children have the condition. The number of cases has mushroomed because of better diagnoses, and a changing definition of autism that includes a broader range of disorders.

Ineffective, Even Dangerous, Treatments

Some of the newer, more popular fad treatments for autism involve special diets or nutritional supplements. Megadoses of Vitamins C and B6 are popular, as well as supplements with fatty acids like omega-3s.

A casein and/or gluten-free diet, which involves eliminating dairy and wheat products, has also gained favor with some parents.

While many of these treatments have never been adequately studied, that doesn't mean they aren't promoted.

"One of the characteristics of fad treatments is that they are discussed in the media and on the internet, where many parents can be exposed to them," said Anne Snow, an Ohio State psychology graduate student.

And while some fads are simply ineffective, others can even be dangerous, Mulick said. Chelation therapy, which involves taking medicines to remove the heavy metal mercury from the body, has reportedly led to the death of at least one autistic boy receiving that treatment. Chelation therapy was also touted years ago as a new treatment against some forms of cancer but was eventually shown to have no helpful effect.

> **FAST FACT**
>
> In a study of twins, it was found that when one twin has autism, the second twin has a 60 percent chance of also being diagnosed with the disorder.

Many parents try multiple approaches, hoping at least one will help. Kettering said one survey she found suggests that the average parent of a child with autism has tried seven different therapies.

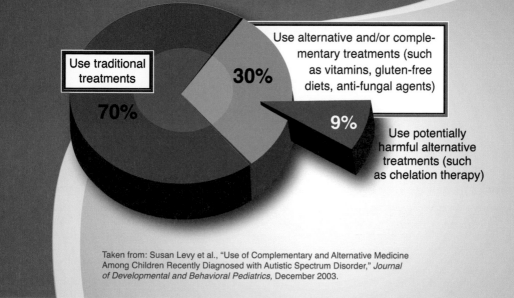

The Use of Alternative Treatments for Autism

The information in this pie chart came from a study that included 284 children recently diagnosed with autism at the Regional Autism Center of the Children's Hospital of Philadelphia, Pennsylvania.

Use traditional treatments

70%

30%

Use alternative and/or complementary treatments (such as vitamins, gluten-free diets, anti-fungal agents)

9%

Use potentially harmful alternative treatments (such as chelation therapy)

Taken from: Susan Levy et al., "Use of Complementary and Alternative Medicine Among Children Recently Diagnosed with Autistic Spectrum Disorder," *Journal of Developmental and Behavioral Pediatrics*, December 2003.

"We're not saying that all of these treatments don't work or that they are all dangerous," Kettering said. "But the research hasn't been done to suggest that most of them are effective or even safe."

Many of the treatments may have just enough basis in scientific fact to attract attention, even if the treatment itself is unproven.

For instance, most scientists believe that many cases of autism are caused by genetic mutations, and some mutations can be caused by various chemicals that we encounter in our everyday lives, Mulick said.

But still, there is no evidence that any particular chemical causes mutations that lead to autism, as some have claimed.

"There's a shred of truth in the rationale presented for some fad treatments, and that is enough for some people to go with," he said.

Another reason that fad treatments persist has to do with the natural course of autism, Mulick said.

A man receives chelation therapy at a clinic in Mexico. Chelation has been shown to be ineffective in treating cancer.

Autism, like many conditions, has cycles in which symptoms get worse and then get better. Parents tend to search for treatments when symptoms are getting worse, and when their children get better—as they do in the normal course of disease—parents credit the new therapy.

"It's natural to have this bias that the therapy you're trying has had some positive effect," he said. "People want to believe."

Traditional Treatment Is Difficult and Expensive

While other treatments are still being investigated, right now the only therapy that has been shown to have a long-term positive effect on autism is called Early Intensive Behavioral Intervention [EIBI], Mulick said.

EIBI is a highly structured approach to learning, in which children with autism are taught first to imitate their teachers. But this treatment is very time-consuming and labor intensive. It involves one-on-one behavioral treatment with the child for up to 40 hours a week for several years.

"It's expensive and difficult for many parents to use," Mulick said. "That's got to be one reason other treatments look attractive to them."

Mulick said other treatments and therapies are being studied. However, it takes years to test treatments for autism because of the nature of the disease and problems with proving effectiveness.

"Autism studies are a long, time-consuming, and expensive process," Mulick said. "And some of the fad treatments being used today would never be approved for testing—they are just too dangerous."

EVALUATING THE AUTHORS' ARGUMENTS:

The author of the previous viewpoint contends that the reason so many more children have autism today than in the past is because of environmental toxins. What reason does James Mulick provide for the increase in autistic children? Whose viewpoint do you think is more persuasive and why? If you were the parent of an autistic child, would you seek alternative treatments? Why or why not?

Chinese Stem Cell Treatments Can Help Treat Childhood Blindness

Wally Kennedy

> *"This is the first case ever—since the Bible—where someone's sight has been restored."*

In the following viewpoint Wally Kennedy tells the story of Dawn and Rylea Barlett. Rylea was born with optic-nerve hypoplasia (ONH), a congenital disease that causes blindness. People with ONH fail to properly develop optic nerves in their eyes. Dawn, Rylea's mother, found out her daughter had ONH when the child was four months old. Each doctor they saw in the United States told Dawn that her daughter would never see. But Dawn would not accept this. She searched the Internet and found a Chinese company that claimed that injections of umbilical cord blood stem cells can help children with ONH grow new optic nerve cells. The U.S. government considers such treatments experimental and unproved, but Dawn chose to take her daughter to China for the stem cell treatments. Dawn now believes the Chinese stem cell treatments have allowed her daughter to see for the first time. Wally Kennedy is a reporter for the *Joplin Globe* of Joplin, Missouri.

AS YOU READ, CONSIDER THE FOLLOWING QUESTIONS:

1. Why does Dawn Barlett say she looked for help for Rylea's condition in countries such as Thailand and India?
2. What is it that Barlett says *umbilical* cord stem cells do not have that *embryonic* stem cells do have, and that enables the umbilical cord stem cells to be used to help develop gray matter?
3. According to Barlett, why did the Chinese doctors say it would take three to six months before they would see any changes in Rylea's eyes?

Rylea Barlett was born blind six years ago today [September 2, 2001]. Her optic nerves did not develop. She was diagnosed when she was a few months old. Doctor after doctor gave her no hope of ever seeing.

On July 4 [2007], the girl received the first of five stem-cell transplants. The stem cells were from umbilical cords. The transplants were done in a remote hospital in China.

Her mother, Dawn Barlett, was told not to expect anything for months. One week after the first transplant, her daughter was responding to the glow of a penlight.

"Three weeks ago on Sunday (Aug. 12 [2007]), she asked me to get the penlight," Barlett said. "She wanted to show me where the light was. She kept grabbing at it. She could see the high contrast."

Then it occurred to Barlett that Rylea might be able to distinguish the features of a person's face.

"I told her I wanted to show her something," Barlett said. "I held my breath and put my face in front of her face. I pulled away and asked her what she saw.

"She said: 'I saw my Mommy. Mommy, you are beautiful.'". . .

Uncharted Territory

For Barlett, the years of continually searching for ways to bring sight to her daughter's hazel eyes, the raising of thousands of dollars through donations, the trip to the other side of the globe and

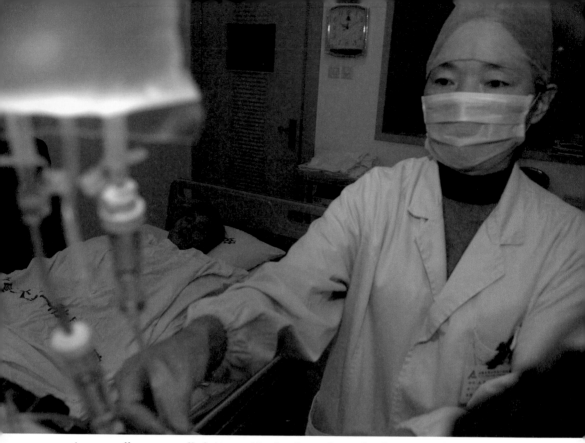

A nurse collects stem cells from an older brother to be used in his younger brother's leukemia treatment.

the unknowns associated with an experimental treatment—at that moment—had all been worth it.

"I started bawling," Barlett said. "She could identify everyone. She had never seen her brother, her sister or me. She had never been able to see—other than to feel—a person's face. She could now put a face with a person.

"What we are seeing now, they did not expect for us to have. We're building nerves."

Rylea could be the first patient anywhere with optic-nerve hypoplasia to benefit from stem-cell transplants from umbilical cords.

Larry Brothers, her optometrist in Joplin, [Missouri,] said: "Her optic nerves did not work. They would not send light back to the brain. People with optic-nerve hypoplasia never develop vision. This is the first case ever—since the Bible—where someone's sight has been restored.

"This is totally uncharted territory. We don't know what to expect. We don't know what the end result will be and whether she will have some functional vision. But two months ago she had nothing, and now she can see light. That's an incredible journey for one small person. It's a miracle."

The Original Diagnosis

After Rylea was born, she had a few medical issues, including a blood-sugar problem, but it did not appear to be serious.

"We did not know anything was wrong until she was 4 months old," Barlett said. "It was in January of 2002. A doctor noticed she wasn't tracking with her eyes. He told us to make an appointment with a pediatric opthalmologist.

"We thought she had a lazy eye. We expected the problem to be minimal. The doctor did an exam. A few minutes later, we are told she is blind and there is nothing we can do to fix it."

Stunned by the news, she sought second, third and fourth opinions.

"It was the same diagnosis everywhere we went," she said. "That's when we took on this whole new world. We were still hopeful, though this was our worst experience with anything bad. We had a perfect baby girl. She was our princess, and something was wrong that no one could fix."

They made trips to Children's Mercy Hospital in Kansas City and other places in search of hope.

"There were a lot of learning experiences," Barlett said. "We never gave up. Her being blind was never OK."

Eventually, Rylea had seen all of the eye specialists her family could find. Brothers continued to see Rylea to check on the health of her eyes, but there was nothing he could do for her.

Brothers and the girl's pediatrician, Dr. Fred Wheeler, of Joplin, were two of the only people to hold out hope for Rylea "when no one else did," Barlett said. "I will never forget what Dr. Wheeler said to me when I talked to him about the stem-cell transplants. He said, 'If there is an answer, this is it.'"

FAST FACT

According to Patients Beyond Borders, more than 150,000 Americans traveled abroad for health care in 2006.

After encountering one wall after another, Barlett became frustrated, but she continued her search on the Internet for promising treatments outside the United States.

"I looked for help in India, Thailand and throughout the world—places where they don't have the FDA (U.S. Food and Drug Administration) to hold back research," she said. "I found this place in China that does umbilical stem-cell transplants."

Barlett Is Concerned for Safety

She sent a brief description of her daughter's condition to the research program in China.

"I knew there was no cure, but at least they were doing research," Barlett said. "I felt there was the possibility of potential improvement for her. I got a response back from a lady in the United States. She was their contact in this country.

"In her letter, she said they had never treated anyone for this condition, but felt there was a significant chance for improvement. For a week to two weeks, I prayed about it. I am not one for false hope. I did not want anything like that."

She put together three pages of questions for her contact.

"I went down the list of possible side effects," she said. "Stem cells can cause tumors. I was concerned about that. But, umbilical-cord stem cells have no antigen markers like embryonic stem cells.

Umbilical-cord stem cells, because of that, can help develop brain and nerve cells—gray matter—but not other things. I thought, 'Maybe they can develop optic-nerve cells.'

"I wanted to know how they did it. Did it involve surgery? I was told she would have intravenous injections and spinal infusions. After weighing the pros and cons, I thought we should try. The only possible side effect was spinal headaches after the procedures. Of course, there was always a possibility of infection."

Barlett found a telephone number for a man in Sikeston [Missouri] who had a spinal-cord injury and had gone to the same Chinese program for stem-cell treatments.

"I wanted to know everything about it, including where it was done and the environment there," she said. "Was the country itself safe? I have never left the United States. This man told me he could not walk, that he was paralyzed from the waist down. When he left there,

Doctors' Opinions About Sending Patients Overseas for Medical Care

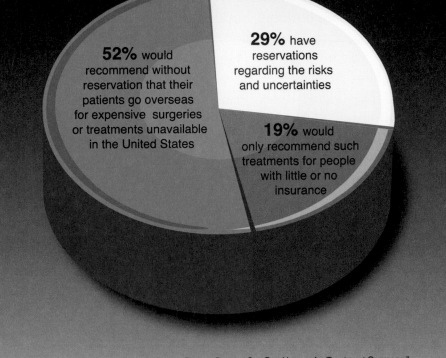

52% would recommend without reservation that their patients go overseas for expensive surgeries or treatments unavailable in the United States

29% have reservations regarding the risks and uncertainties

19% would only recommend such treatments for people with little or no insurance

Taken from: Marianne Mattera, "Survey Report: Doctors Say Bon Voyage for Treatment Overseas," *Med Page Today*, August 24, 2007. www.medpagetoday.com.

he had sweating in his legs and could move his toes for the first time. He still wasn't able to walk, but some small things had improved. That was the confirmation I needed."

On Jan. 1 [2007], Barlett created a Web site telling her daughter's story. The fund raising for the trip to China began. Donation cans were set up in convenience stores. A benefit golf tournament was held. A family member in Chicago organized a union benefit. One man donated 120,000 airline miles for the round-trip tickets.

The Journey for a Treatment

They flew from Chicago to Shanghai. It was a 15-hour flight.

"We went to Hangzhou, which is a three- to four-hour drive from Shanghai," Barlett said. "I kept thinking, 'What are we doing?' Every billboard was in Chinese. People were working in rice fields. What are we doing here? There was the culture shock part of it, but I was not scared. It seemed that every door we encountered opened."

They stayed in a hotel that was four blocks from the hospital.

"It was a modern building, but the hospital was very different from what we are used to," she said.

"There was no HIPAA [Health Insurance Portability and Accountability Act] (medical privacy act). Lots of people were in your business. They called Rylea 'Princess' because to them, she looked like a Barbie doll. She got hugs and kisses because she stood out with her long, blondish-brown hair. I never felt like these people were put out. They were very willing to help."

They arrived on July 1.

"Her first stem-cell transplant was done by IV [intravenously] on July 4," Barlett said. "It was symbolic for us because it was the beginning of her independence.

"They said it would be three to six months before we would see any changes. It takes that much time for stem cells to mature and become connectors. A week later, on July 11, she started responding to light. Before, when you put a penlight to her eyes, her pupils would not contract when light was shined in them.

"When the doctor shined the light in her eyes, she shut her eyes and turned away. The doctor looked at me. We looked at each other. Everyone was completely silent. In broken English, the doctor says, 'Congratulations.' I started bawling."

Rylea had three spinal transplants and another IV transplant before they left the hospital. Each transplant involved 10 million cells. The trip and treatments were financed by nearly $40,000 in donations.

After they returned to the United States on July 30, they met with Brothers so he could assess the girl's progress.

As Rylea Improves, the Barletts Help Others

"We were hoping she would give us some reaction to light," Barlett said. "She not only saw the light, she saw a chart across the room with a big 'E' on it. He determined that she has 20/400 vision.

"I will never forget Dr. Brothers saying: 'We have never had numbers. Do you realize we have never had numbers?' He was so excited."

The plan now is to go back to China in March [2008] for another round of stem-cell transplants.

"She will not get 100 percent vision from this, but you continue to build on what you have gained," Barlett said.

Now that the whirlwind trip to China is over, life is returning to normal for Rylea and her sister, Kyra, 4, and brother, Zack, 12. But the trip has opened a whole new dimension for their mother.

"The parents of children with optic-nerve hypoplasia have seen her Web site and the progress she has made, and we're getting thousands and thousands of e-mails, comments and phone calls," Barlett said. "You want to help every one of them. You want to offer families hope because we know what it is like to not have any hope."

EVALUATING THE AUTHOR'S ARGUMENTS:

This viewpoint tells the personal account of Dawn and Rylea Barlett. Can you think of something about personal anecdotes that may make them particularly persuasive? Think about Dawn's description of when her daughter saw her face for the first time.

Chinese Stem Cell Treatments Are Unpredictable and Risky

Mark Borchert, interviewed by Joe Neel

"Most children do not have a miraculous improvement. A child will not go from light perception to 20/40 vision or driving vision or reading vision."

In the following viewpoint Joe Neel interviews Mark Borchert and asks him to discuss optic-nerve hypoplasia (ONH), one of the most common causes of childhood blindness. Borchert says that ONH does not just cause blindness. It also causes hormone and development problems. Children with ONH typically have ill-functioning pituitary glands, learning disabilities, and speech and communications issues. Borchert has problems with Chinese stem cell therapies purporting to treat ONH. He contends that these treatments are risky, unproven, and unethical. According to Borchert, there is no scientific evidence to prove that Chinese treatments work, and innocent children are being used for research. Borchert is the head of the vision center at Children's Hospital, Los Angeles.

Joe Neel and Mark Borchert, "Childhood Blindness: What Are the Options?" NPR, March 18, 2008. Reproduced by permission.

AS YOU READ, CONSIDER THE FOLLOWING QUESTIONS:
1. According to Borchert, what percentage of children with ONH also have abnormal function of their pituitary gland?
2. According to Borchert, if children could be diagnosed by neonatal-screening tests, what types of problems could be prevented?
3. Borchert says that there is no peer-reviewed scientific evidence that cord-blood stem cells can ever do what?

Some U.S. experts say there is no evidence that the stem-cell therapy being offered in China will work in one of the most common causes of childhood blindness, optic-nerve hypoplasia (ONH). We asked Dr. Mark Borchert, head of the vision center at Children's Hospital Los Angeles, to explain more about the disease and possible treatments.

What is ONH?

Optic-nerve hypoplasia is a failure of development of the optic nerves of one or both eyes. It's associated with the failure of development of the connections of the neurons with parts of the brain. ONH is a major cause of congenital blindness in children.

What causes it?

We do not know what causes it. We know that it is almost certainly not genetic.

Is it on the rise?

Most of us in pediatric ophthalmology who see a lot of children with congenital blindness think it's increasing in frequency. We don't have good statistics in the U.S. on the prevalence of vision loss in children. But statistics from Europe, especially the Scandinavian countries, show it is the only cause of visual impairment—congenital visual impairment—that is actually increasing. All the other causes are decreasing. But we don't have good information for the U.S.

ONH is not just blindness, is it?

Not at all. It's a brain-development problem. Children with optic-nerve hypoplasia have a whole host of systemic and neurological

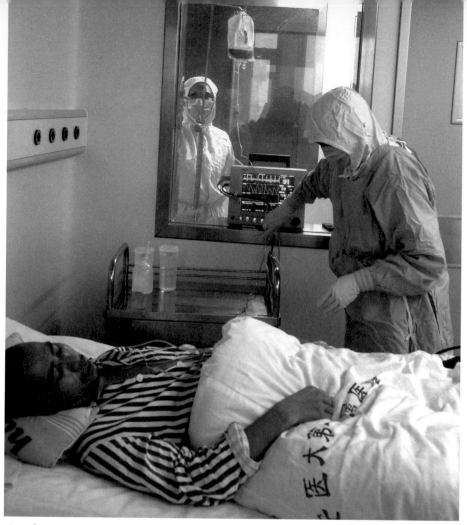

A male patient undergoes a stem cell transplant operation in China. The author contends that China's treatment program is risky and unethical.

problems. The most obvious are problems in controlling the pituitary gland, which controls most of the hormones in the body, including sex hormones, growth hormone, steroid hormones for your body to deal with stress, thyroid hormone, and anti-diuretic hormone. Of these children with ONH, about 80 percent have abnormal function of their pituitary gland and ultimately need some sort of treatment with replacement hormones.

In addition to that, children with ONH have a lot of developmental problems—learning disabilities, motor disabilities and speech and communication problems. And these often don't become apparent until the child is a little older, sometimes long after the diagnosis of optic-nerve hypoplasia has been made.

Does treating the hormone problems help with vision?

We don't know the answer to that. We're in the process of studying that right now. There's certainly a suggestion that early recognition and treatment of some of the hormone problems leads to better outcomes—in particular, early recognition and treatment of the thyroid-hormone deficiency. However, the children with optic-nerve hypoplasia have thyroid-hormone dysfunction due to a problem with the hypothalamus that controls the pituitary gland. And hypothyroidism due to this is not picked up with the current neonatal-screening procedures.

Consequently, the hypothyroidism in these children is not detected until after the optic-nerve hypoplasia is detected, and that is usually when the child is old enough for the parents and doctors to recognize that there's a vision problem. That's usually at several months of age and is too late to prevent the major effects of hypothyroidism. Presumably, if you could diagnose them earlier with a better neonatal-screening test you could prevent a lot of the cognitive and intelligence problems that afflict these children. We're also doing studies on whether or not early treatment with thyroid hormone or growth hormone impacts their vision development or their cognitive development as well as their growth.

FAST FACT

The stem cell company Beike Biotech says each year about three thousand people suffering from debilitating diseases pay twenty thousand to thirty thousand dollars each for stem cell treatments in China.

What happens in children who are getting an experimental treatment?

We currently know that regardless of whether or not they are treated, at least 50 percent of children get some improvement up until five years of age. We don't know whether they can improve beyond that.

So it's hard to tell if a treatment is working or if they're just improving naturally?

Absolutely, and that's why a controlled study needs to be done, such as we're doing with the growth-hormone study. We're trying to

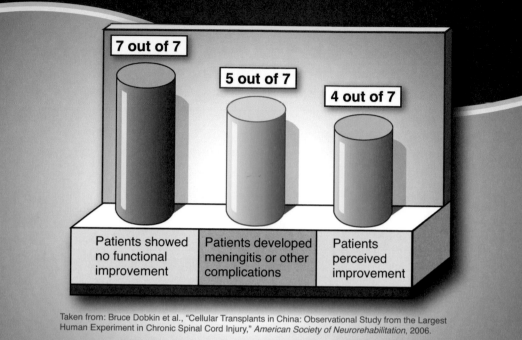

The Results of Seven Patients Receiving Experimental Chinese Treatments for Spinal Cord Injuries

7 out of 7

5 out of 7

4 out of 7

| Patients showed no functional improvement | Patients developed meningitis or other complications | Patients perceived improvement |

Taken from: Bruce Dobkin et al., "Cellular Transplants in China: Observational Study from the Largest Human Experiment in Chronic Spinal Cord Injury," *American Society of Neurorehabilitation*, 2006.

determine whether it's the growth hormone that's actually improving their vision beyond what they would normally improve.

In those who do improve, how much better is their vision?
Most children do not have a miraculous improvement. A child will not go from light perception to 20/40 vision or driving vision or reading vision. That would be extremely unusual. However, it is extremely common for children to go from no light perception or bare light perception to being able to see very large objects, such as automobiles, or being able to navigate around a room without a cane or a dog.

What are you telling parents who are asking about the Chinese stem-cell therapy?
That I have two problems with this therapy.

First, from a scientific point of view, there is no evidence that cord-blood stem cells can ever form neurons, at least not in any peer-reviewed scientific literature. And I can assure you anyone doing legitimate research in this area is not withholding information to the contrary, because obviously this would be a major breakthrough if neurons could form from cord-blood stem cells.

Even if they could form neurons, there's no evidence that these neurons could ever make it to the eye where they could form new ganglion cells that are the cells that form the optic nerve, because the eye is a very protected environment from foreign material.

Second, from an ethical point of view, it is really not appropriate to be treating children who cannot give assent to the procedure themselves with a therapy that has no basis even in the laboratory for its use. Also, there are real risks with any procedure in which you are injecting foreign material into the body, especially if you're injecting it into the cerebrospinal fluid, which is my understanding of what they're doing in China. Because this foreign material can cause inflammation, can cause meningitis and cause serious brain injury.

It's also an ethical problem because I do not think that thorough and formal consent is obtained.

Finally, there's no scientific oversight of this work. In this country and Europe, this type of research could never be done without scientific oversight, even making sure that they're actually doing what they say they're doing. There is no way of knowing that they're actually purifying stem cells appropriately, that they're injecting stem cells, that they have any sort of monitoring of adverse effects from this. So this is really an inappropriate way to do any research, especially on innocent children.

EVALUATING THE AUTHOR'S ARGUMENTS:

What scientific merit do you think Mark Borchert would assign to the anecdotal evidence presented in the previous viewpoint? Do you think Borchert would think differently about Chinese stem cell treatments if his child had ONH? If you had a devastating illness, would you travel to another country for experimental treatment? Was your opinion changed by either of the viewpoints? Why or why not?

Chapter 3

What Role Should Alternative Medicine Play in Health Care in the United States?

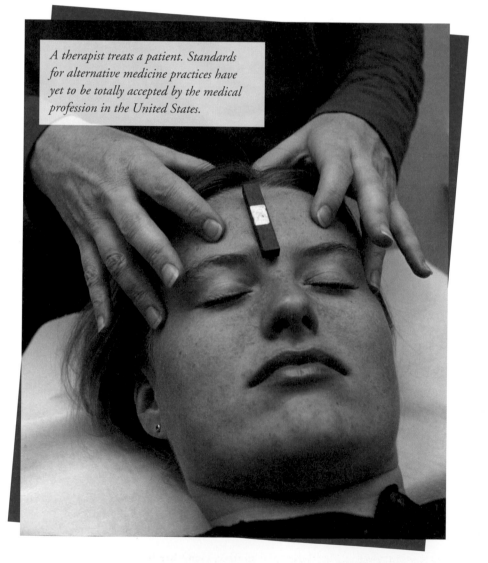

A therapist treats a patient. Standards for alternative medicine practices have yet to be totally accepted by the medical profession in the United States.

There Are Many Definitions of Alternative Medicine in the United States

Committee on the Use of Complementary and Alternative Medicine by the American Public

"This discussion of definitions shows that no clear and consistent definition of CAM exists."

The following viewpoint is an excerpt from a report about complementary and alternative medicine (CAM), which was written by an expert committee assembled by the U.S. Institute of Medicine (IOM). The committee was asked to do a study about CAM use in the United States. According to the committee, in order to study CAM, they needed to come up with an acceptable definition of what CAM is. The committee found that there are many different definitions of CAM. Some definitions describe CAM as being merely different than mainstream medicine, while other definitions try to list all the different types of CAM. In the end, the committee settled on a broad definition of CAM that allows for change and incorporates practices that may not have evidence of effectiveness but that patients perceive as being effective. The Institute of Medicine was established in 1970 to provide objective, scientifically based medical advice to the U.S. government. The CAM committee comprised over a dozen doctors and medical professors from all over the United States.

AS YOU READ, CONSIDER THE FOLLOWING QUESTIONS:
1. How many different potential CAM therapies, practices, or systems did the New York State Office of Regulatory Reform and CAM identify, according to the committee?
2. According to the committee, the National Center for Complementary and Alternative Medicine (NCCAM) divides CAM methods into five different categories. What types of therapies or methods are included in the third category?
3. The committee stated that there were several reasons it chose the definition of CAM that it did. What was the committee's third reason for choosing its definition?

One of the difficulties in any study of CAM [complementary and alternative medicine] is trying to determine what is included in the definition of CAM. Does CAM include vitamin use, nutrition and diets, behavioral medicine, exercise and other treatments that have been integrated into conventional medical systems? Should CAM include prayer, shamanism, or other therapies that may not be considered health care practices? . . . The reasons for defining modalities as "CAM therapies" are not only scientific but also "political, social, [and] conceptual" [according to Wayne B. Jonas]. In the United States, some of the most frequently used and well-known therapies that are recognized as CAM are relaxation techniques, herbs, chiropractic, and massage therapy. Chiropractic, acupuncture, and massage therapy are licensed in most states. Naturopathy and homeopathy are licensed in fewer states, Numerous other therapies and modalities are considered unlicensed practices and at present few or no formal regulations apply to these therapies and modalities. The New York State Office of Regulatory Reform and CAM has identified more than 100 therapies, practices, and systems that could be considered CAM.

A New Definition Is Needed

A lack of consistency in the definition of what is included in CAM is found throughout the literature. The National Center for Complementary and Alternative Medicine (NCCAM) of NIH [the National Institutes of Health] defines CAM as "a group of diverse medical and health care systems, practices, and products that are not presently considered to be part of conventional medicine." However, many would argue that a therapy does not cease to be a CAM therapy because it has been proven to be safe and effective and is used in conventional practice. "Simply because an herbal remedy comes to be used by physicians does not mean that herbalists cease to practice, or that the practice of the one becomes like that of the other" [according to David J. Hufford].

Descriptive definitions of CAM include one by [CAM professor Edzard] Ernst, who write[s] that CAM is a "diagnosis, treatment and/or prevention which complements mainstream medicine by contributing to a common whole, satisfying a demand not met by orthodox, or diversifying the conceptual framework of medicine." [Medical historian Norman] Gevitz proposes that CAM include "practices that are not accepted as correct, proper, or appropriate or are not in conformity with the beliefs or standards of the dominant group of medical practitioners in a society." In 1993, [Harvard CAM professor David] Eisenberg defined CAM as "interventions neither taught widely in medical schools nor generally available in hospitals."

Mainstream Medicine and CAM Are Not Mutually Exclusive

[Professor of medical humanities Loretta] Kopelman argues that descriptive definitions such as those offered by Ernst and Gevitz do not adequately answer the question, What is CAM? Definitions that place CAM outside the politically dominant health care system fail "to offer a standard for differentiating conventional interventions and CAM other than by appealing to what is or is not intrinsic to the practices of the dominant culture. This assumes there is a reliable and useful way to count cultures or subcultures and sort them into those that are dominant and those that are not." Other descriptive definitions fail because conditions change, and therefore, descriptions of the conditions are no longer accurate. For example, look at the definition of Eisenberg and colleagues, which states that CAM comprises interventions that are neither taught widely in medical schools nor generally available in hospitals; however, more than half of all U.S. medical schools provide education about CAM, health care institutions are offering CAM services, and the numbers of insurers offering reimbursement for CAM therapies is growing.

According to Kopelman, normative definitions (e.g., untested or unscientific) also fail to distinguish CAM from conventional medicine. For example, [Marcia Angell and Jerome P. Kassier] write "there is only medicine that has been adequately tested and medicine that has not." However, such a definition does not distinguish between conventional medicine and CAM because many conventional treatments have not been supported by rigorous testing. For example, a review of . . . the effectiveness of conventional biomedical procedures [by Jeanette Ezzo] found that 20 percent showed no effect, whereas insufficient evidence was available for another 21 percent. Furthermore, [according to Kopelma,] "some CAM manufacturers adopt higher standards than are currently required in the United States and rigorously test their CAM products."

Stipulative definitions (i.e., lists of therapies) are not successful in distinguishing CAM from conventional therapies, Kopelman argues,

A patient undergoes hot stones therapy, which is one of many types of complementary and alternative medicine treatments that is practiced in the United States.

because they are not consistent from source to source and they provide no justification for the exclusion of therapies that are not included.

Attempts to Classify

Given the lack of a consistent definition of CAM, some have tried to bring clarity to the situation by proposing classification systems that can be used to organize the field. One of the most widely used classification structures, developed by NCCAM, divides CAM modalities into five categories:

1. Alternative medical systems,
2. Mind-body interventions,
3. Biologically based treatments,
4. Manipulative and body-based methods, and
5. Energy therapies.

As the name implies, alternative medical systems is a category that extends beyond a single modality, and refers to an entire system of theory and practice that developed separately from conventional medicine. Examples of these systems include traditional Chinese medicine, ayurvedic medicine, homeopathy, and naturopathy.

The second category in the NCCAM classification scheme is mind-body interventions, which include practices that are based on the human mind, but that have an effect on the human body and physical health, such as meditation, prayer, and mental healing.

The third category, biologically based therapies, includes specialized diets, herbal products, and other natural products such as minerals, hormones, and biologicals. Specialized diets include those proposed by Drs. Atkins and Ornish, as well as the broader field of functional foods that may reduce the risk of disease or promote health. A few of the well-known herbals for which there is evidence of effectiveness include St. John's wort for the treatment of mild to moderate depression and *Ginkgo biloba* for the treatment of mild cognitive impairment. An example of a nonherbal natural product is fish oil for the treatment of cardiovascular conditions.

The fourth category, manipulative and body-based methods, includes therapies that involve movement or manipulation of the body. Chiropractic is the best known in this category, and chiropractors are licensed to practice in every U.S. state. A defining feature of

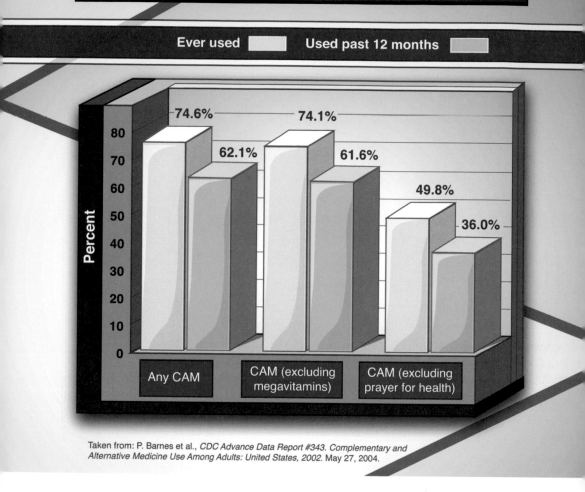

Complementary and Alternative Medicine (CAM) Use by Adults in the United States, 2002

Ever used ☐   Used past 12 months ☐

74.6%   74.1%

62.1%   61.6%

49.8%

36.0%

Percent: 80, 70, 60, 50, 40, 30, 20, 10, 0

Any CAM   CAM (excluding megavitamins)   CAM (excluding prayer for health)

Taken from: P. Barnes et al., *CDC Advance Data Report #343. Complementary and Alternative Medicine Use Among Adults: United States, 2002.* May 27, 2004.

chiropractic treatment is spinal manipulation, also known as spinal adjustment, to correct spinal joint abnormalities. Massage therapy is another example of a body-based therapy.

The final category described by NCCAM is energy therapies which include the manipulation and application of energy fields to the body. In addition to electromagnetic fields outside of the body, it is hypothesized that energy fields exist within the body. The existence of these biofields has not been experimentally proven; however, a number of therapies include them, such as qi gong, Reiki, and therapeutic touch.

A different approach to classifying CAM modalities, [described by Eisenberg and his colleagues,] is a descriptive taxonomy that groups therapies according to their philosophical and theoretical identities. Practices are divided into two groups. The first group appeals to the general public and has become popularly known as CAM. This group includes professionalized or distinct medical systems (e.g., chiropractic, acupuncture, homeopathy), popular health reform (e.g., dietary supplement use and specialized diets), New Age healing (e.g., qi gong, Reiki, magnets), psychological interventions, and nonnormative scientific enterprises (conventional therapies used in unconventional ways or unconventional therapies used by conventionally trained medical or scientific professionals). The second group includes practices that are more relevant to specific populations, such as ethnic or religious groups (e.g., Native American traditional medicine, Puerto Rican spiritism, folk medicine, and religious healing).

A Working Definition

This discussion of definitions shows that no clear and consistent definition of CAM exists, nor is there a recognized taxonomy to organize the field, although the one proposed by NCCAM is commonly used. Given the committee's charge and focus, for the purposes of this report, the committee has chosen to use as its working definition of CAM a modification of the definition

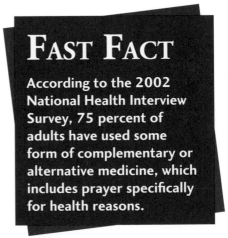

proposed by the Panel on Definition and Description at a 1995 NIH research methodology conference. This modified definition states that

> Complementary and alternative medicine (CAM) is a broad domain of resources that encompasses health systems, modalities, and practices and their accompanying theories and beliefs, other than those intrinsic to the dominant health system of a particular society or culture in a given historical period. CAM includes such resources perceived by their users as associated with positive health outcomes. Boundaries within CAM and between the CAM domain and the domain of the dominant system are not always sharp or fixed.

The committee chose this definition for several reasons. First, this broad definition reflects the scope and essence of CAM as used by the American public. Second, it avoids excluding common practices from the research agenda. . . . The third reason for choosing to define CAM as stated above is that it is patient centered and includes practices that people perceive to have health benefits. Fourth, it encompasses the potential for change. That is, this definition allows a therapy to be accepted as standard practice when there is evidence of effectiveness but still allows the therapy to remain a part of CAM. Furthermore, the chosen definition recognizes that the definition of "conventional" medicine will vary from time to time and from country to country, it does not presume that proven practices will be adopted, and it allows CAM to be evaluated over time.

EVALUATING THE AUTHOR'S ARGUMENTS:

In this viewpoint the Institute of Medicine expert committee on CAM describes the process it went through in order to choose a particular working definition of CAM. Do you believe they have made a good choice of a CAM definition? Why or why not? Would you have chosen a different definition? Do you think they did a good job of supporting their choice of a CAM definition? Explain.

Alternative Medicine Has a Lot in Common with Mainstream American Medicine

John Gamel

In the following viewpoint John Gamel contends that complementary and alternative medicine (CAM) has a lot in common with mainstream medicine. Gamel says the placebo effect is the key to what connects the two theories of medicine. Gamel contends that CAM relies almost entirely on the placebo effect. However, he points out that many mainstream treatments were—and perhaps still are—based on people's believing they feel better, even though the scientific evidence shows the treatment really did not help their ailments. Gamel says most people today go to the doctor because of old age, unhealthy lifestyles, or stress-related illnesses. These are things that are

John Gamel, "Hokum on the Rise: The 70-Percent Solution," *Antioch Review,* Winter 2008. Copyright © 2008 by the Antioch Review, Inc. Reproduced by permission of the editors.

hard for mainstream medicine to cure. However, CAM is excellent in this regard. Gamel believes the key to CAM's success is human nature: we believe what we want, or perhaps what we need, to believe. Gamel is an author and professor emeritus of ophthalmology at the University of Louisville School of Medicine.

AS YOU READ, CONSIDER THE FOLLOWING QUESTIONS:
1. According to Gamel, what was the reported improvement rate for the LIMA procedure?
2. Gamel says that mainstream doctors used to measure truth by the same criterion used by alternative medicine practitioners today. What is this criterion?
3. Who is Deepak Chopra, according to the author?

Julian Howell, the family doctor who cared for me during my childhood in Selma, Alabama, had an impish smile and a garrulous, backslapping charm that soothed the most anxious patient. A few years after my graduation from medical school, when Julian was approaching retirement, I stopped by his home for a visit. We sat on his back patio, a broad expanse of terra cotta tiles shaded by a canopy of oaks and sycamores. A fountain fed by an artesian well gurgled nearby. In the purple twilight of a summer evening, as doctors are so often wont to do, we drifted through a long, pleasant swapping of medical tales. I strutted my nascent expertise by citing the triumph of my internship, a gentleman whose chronic blood loss I had diagnosed within five minutes of his admission to Santa Clara Valley Medical Center by testing his stool for occult blood. Months of seepage from a gastric ulcer had left the poor man profoundly anemic. He was pale as a ghost.

When Julian's turn came, he sipped his bourbon on the rocks, set it down on the glass table between us, then swore that the palest creature the world had ever seen was Amantha Hargood, a ten-year-old patient he had examined many years before.

"I spun down her blood right then and there," Julian said. "The hematocrit was twelve, I wanted to put her in the hospital, but her parents didn't have a pot to piss in, couldn't come near affording the twenty dollars a day it cost back then. They sharecropped a little plot out by Marion Junction, fed her mostly corn—corn mush, corn bread, a scrap of fatback every now and then. Her skin was so pale you could almost see her bones."

But Amantha suffered from more than anemia. She was cachectic [weak and thin], short for her age, with limbs thin and frail as a spider's. Her joints were swollen. Her gums bled all the time, tinting her saliva pink, and a mass of bruises ran all the way up her bony spine. The father told a disturbing story.

A New Treatment Improves On the Old

"Well, Amantha's been doing right poorly for more'n a year, so a while back we got holt of this preacher over in Uniontown. He came to the house, charged a dollar an hour to read the New Testament while he sat in Amantha's room resting his hand on her head. Cost us four dollars to get through Matthew and Mark, but halfway through Luke we decided she wasn't getting much better, so we took her to Doc Jensen." (Jensen, a Selma chiropractor, lived in an antebellum mansion famous for the cannonball hole blasted through one of its Greek Revival columns during the Civil War.) "Jensen told us Amantha had a collapsed colon and made us sign up for five treatments, charged six dollars on the spot, but that first treatment raised all them bruises up and down her back. When the time come for her next treatment, she squalled so loud we just give up. Finally things got so bad we decided we'd best get us a real doctor."

Julian diagnosed scurvy, a deficiency of vitamin C that stunts growth, impairs healing, and causes patients to bruise and bleed easily. He also diagnosed protein deficiency and iron deficiency anemia. He gave Amantha injections of vitamin C and ferrous sulfate, then instructed the parents to supplement her daily diet with one pork chop, the juice of a fresh orange, and over-the-counter iron tablets. When they brought her back a month later, the bleeding and bruising were gone. She had gained twelve pounds. Julian claims—I tend to doubt this, despite his famous veracity—she had already grown a head taller.

He charged the Hargoods a dollar for each of the two visits.

"Thank you, doctor," the father said. "We're glad we came."

Deepak Chopra began his medical career in traditional medicine but now advocates almost every form of alternative medicine.

Julian Howell, god rest his sweet soul, was the gentlest man I ever knew, but he loathed chiropractors. Every time the subject was mentioned, Julian's impish smile vanished. His face grew dark with rage. It does something to a doctor when a farmer with metastatic bone cancer limps into his office carrying a basket of fresh-picked corn in lieu of payment because the farmer's savings have been drained by a high-school graduate with six months of training at the Alabama Chiropractic College. Indeed, chiropractors have inflicted upon modern medicine some of its most humiliating defeats. . . .

CAM and Mainstream Medicine Are Alleged Enemies

Julian's long life ended two decades ago, just before the rising onslaught of what is now called CAM—Complementary and

Alternative Medicine. Since then, unorthodox therapies have gained a wider audience with each passing day, even in such exalted institutions as Harvard and Johns Hopkins. From Maine to California, in shopping malls and store-front boutiques, CAM practitioners offer yoga, acupuncture, iridology, naturopathy, massage therapy, aroma therapy, and colonic infusions of coffee extracted from organically grown, high caffeine beans. In some of the more eclectic venues, the shaman who reads your palm will also soothe your irritable bowel with whiffs of lavender and patchouli oil.

In theory, CAM and modern medicine remain very much at war. Of the various remedies popular across the tides of human history, only a tiny faction have been incorporated into the discipline we call "modern," "mainstream," or "scientific" medicine. This is not to say that only science can relieve suffering. Indeed, all popular treatments "work"—that is, they make patients feel better. Otherwise they wouldn't be popular. The scientists who rail against CAM often overlook this crucial point: if something makes a profit in the open market, be it a pill or a Barbie Doll, then by definition it works. Medical purists grumble about placebos and biologic mechanisms, while CAM practitioners laugh all the way to the bank. What patient gives a hoot for biologic mechanisms so long as those tingly acupuncture needles relieve a backache that has tormented him for weeks?

The Staggering Power of the Placebo

In the annals of medicine, 1960 became a landmark year when David Sabiston and Alfred Blalock, distinguished professors at Johns Hopkins University, published the results of a controversial clinical trial. Especially disturbing was the fact that anyone dared conduct such a trial, since the procedure it tested, ligation of the internal mammary artery (LIMA), had already been performed on hundreds of patients with coronary artery disease, and respected surgeons had reported an improvement rate that approached 70 percent. Most victims obtained at least partial relief from chest pain, and some even showed objective signs of benefit, such as changes toward normal in their electrocardiogram.

Undeterred by these results, Sabiston and Blalock conducted what many regarded as a horrific experiment: thirty-four patients were randomly divided into two groups, and, while the first group received a standard LIMA, the second group was subjected to a sham procedure that left them with the same surgical scar, so neither the patients nor their cardiologists knew who had received the real operation. The first group showed the expected results: chest pain was relieved in 70 percent, exercise tolerance increased, many were able to return to work, and some showed objective improvement in their EKG [electrocardiogram]. Sabiston and Blalock were saved from the academic equivalent of a lynch mob only because the sham-operated group displayed the same benefit, revealing for all to see the staggering power of the placebo effect.

Subsequent research has proved this study to be more the rule than the exception. When surgeries and medicines are tested in an informal setting—that is, a setting that does not control for psychological factors or statistical bias—the great majority seem to be effective. Yet, tragically, when proper scientific scrutiny is finally brought to bear, these same treatments are often shown to be worthless or even harmful. Sometimes this scrutiny comes too late to save thousands from unnecessary suffering, disfigurement, or death. . . .

The Two Types of Medicine Share a Common Goal

At the core of the conflict between scientific and alternative medicine lies a marvelous irony. Until recent decades, mainstream physicians measured truth by the same criterion used today by alternative practitioners: did the treatment make the patient feel better? To be sure, physicians in bygone eras often based their preliminary decisions—decisions about what remedies should be tried in an effort to heal the patient of a particular illness—on what was thought at the time to be scientific evidence, but conclusions as to what actually worked were based on that magical moment when the patient told the doctor how he felt after the treatment. And this moment, as has been amply shown, falls easy prey to bias, random noise, regression to the mean, and a variety of psychological factors. Thus CAM follows closely in the footsteps of what was once regarded as mainstream medicine—a discipline whose exemplars, until recent decades, judged treatments by the same criteria now espoused by naturopaths, chiropractors, acupuncturists, and aroma therapists: if the patient feels better, the treatment works.

On occasion, a useless or harmful therapy persists for many years because the doctors, not the patients, are convinced of its benefit. Generations of ophthalmologists treated traumatic hyphema (a hemorrhage within the eye) by patching both eyes and putting the patient at absolute bed rest (that is, no ambulation whatsoever) for as long as a week. The origins of this gruesome regimen are lost in history, but it seemed to make sense: by restricting the patient's eye movements, patching should reduce the risk of further hemorrhage, which could lead to blinding complications.

In 1973, after decades of unquestioning devotion to an undocumented historical precedent, eye doctors around the world were shocked when investigators at a South African hospital dared to perform a controlled clinical trial. Half the patients suffering a traumatic hyphema were treated with patching plus bed rest, while the other half were allowed to lead normal lives. Since this radical experiment denied half the patients a treatment considered ophthalmology's Holy Grail, a cry of alarm went up, but the villains became heroes when the two treatment groups showed identical outcomes. By discrediting an ineffective therapy, these bold investigators saved thousands of future patients from needless torment.

Even more disturbing is the history of episiotomy, a surgical incision made to enlarge the mother's birth canal during delivery. For decades, many obstetricians performed an episiotomy on every patient, hoping with a single clean incision to avoid spontaneous tears that would be more difficult to repair. They also thought the procedure would help women avoid incontinence and improve their sexual response, though no scientific evidence supported either conclusion. Thousands of women were subjected to this operation before an extensive review published in 2005 by the *Journal of the American Medical Association* showed that routine episiotomy increases the risk of pain, injury, and delayed healing following childbirth.

> ## FAST FACT
>
> According to the National Ambulatory Medical Care Survey, in 2006 about 50 percent of visits to doctors' offices were made by patients with chronic conditions such as high blood pressure (22 percent), arthritis (13 percent), high cholesterol (13 percent), diabetes (9.5 percent), and depression (8 percent).

Perceptive Evidence, as Well as Scientific Evidence, Can Be Important

From such alarming histories, it becomes clear that alternative and mainstream medicine once followed parallel paths, basing their tenets on the biased impressions of therapists and patients rather than on objective evidence. The parting of ways came only when medical scientists discovered the true magnitude of the placebo effect and began formulating the rigorous adjustments in experimental design necessary to root out its impact on both the doctor and the patient. . . .

On the positive side, such rigor has allowed medicine to focus its resources on truly effective therapies, therapies that have led to a substantial improvement in the prognosis for crippling and life-threatening diseases. These diseases, however, affect only a small fraction of patients, while the remaining patients—those who suffer from psychosomatic disorders, routine viral infections, the effects of age and lifestyle, and a host of other untreatable or nearly unbeatable maladies—may find the scientific approach less than satisfactory. Perhaps nothing can be done to keep such patients away from quackery [allegedly false medicine]. Perhaps we should not try. Many will suffer injury at the hands of a shaman who can't distinguish a ganglion cell from a fibroblast, but against such failings we must set two important factors: the often compelling psychological benefit of the shaman's placebos, versus the complications a doctor might cause by prescribing unneeded drugs in an effort to please his patient. . . .

CAM Practitioners Are Infiltrating Mainstream Medicine

Powerful indeed are the ties that bind CAM to the fallible traditions of mainstream medicine. Only in the past few decades have medical curricula expanded to include the rigorous standards of controlled clinical trials. Furthermore, many practicing physicians ignore or reject the subtleties of scientific reason, leaving themselves vulnerable to the placebo's seductive lure. Deepak Chopra, perhaps the wealthiest and most famous of America's CAM practitioners, began his career well within the bounds of traditional medicine by serving as chief of staff at Boston Regional Medical Center and by teaching at Tufts University and Boston University Schools of Medicine. Now thoroughly seduced by the placebo effect, he is the author of thirty-five books plus one hundred audio, video, and CD-ROM titles that advocate virtually every form of alternative therapy.

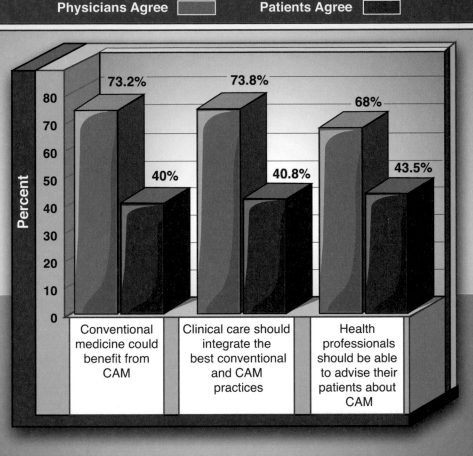

Doctor and Patient Attitudes About Complementary and Alternative Medicine (CAM)

Physicians Agree ▢   **Patients Agree** ▢

Percent

- Conventional medicine could benefit from CAM: 73.2% / 40%
- Clinical care should integrate the best conventional and CAM practices: 73.8% / 40.8%
- Health professionals should be able to advise their patients about CAM: 68% / 43.5%

Taken from: Mandi L. Furlow et al., "Physician and Patient Attitudes Towards Complementary and Alternative Medicine in Obstetrics and Gynecology," *BMC Complementary and Alternative Medicine*, 2008.

Despite these non-standard credentials, Chopra remains an instructor at such exalted institutions as the University of California School of Medicine, Harvard Medical School, and Beth Israel Deaconess Medical Center. It seems appropriate that Chopra and legions of his ilk should now populate the halls of academic medicine, since they carry on the placebo-dominated traditions long ago established in those very halls by their progenitors, respected professors whose measure of success differed not one jot from the measure used nowadays by iridologists, chiropractors, and massage therapists.

Purists rage and splutter, arguing that science, not the archaic mumbo jumbo of voodoo and witchcraft, has given us immunizations, antibiotics, antisepsis, anesthesia, modern surgery, etc.—a panoply of benefits that over the last century has increased the life expectancy of Americans from forty-seven to seventy-seven years. This argument is sound. Whatever psychological comfort patients may derive from herbal nostrums or touchy-feely therapies, only a handful of properly controlled trials have demonstrated an unequivocal benefit from the hundreds of alternative treatments offered around the globe. Thus while CAM has moved backward by promoting remedies that are ancient and unproven—or, in some cases, ancient and proven to be worthless—modern medicine has saved hundreds of thousands of patients, many of them children, from an agonizing premature death.

Human Nature Makes Us Believe in CAM

And yet, despite their sound logic and noble ambitions, I suspect that scientists will fail in their efforts to expunge CAM from the landscape of American medicine. The cause of this failure is rooted in human nature, as I discovered some years ago while attending a convention sponsored by the Committee for Scientific Investigation of Claims of the Paranormal. CSICOP was founded by a panel of gifted scientists, magicians, and psychologists who devote their lives to defending science against pseudoscientific nonsense. As one might expect, my fellow attendees were a skeptical lot, but they remained vulnerable to a human and all too common frailty. I explored this frailty by conducting an informal clinical trial of my own during the dinners and cocktail parties that followed each day's lectures.

Several times each evening, after striking up a conversation with a randomly selected male, I asked my subject whether he was married. If he answered in the affirmative, and if his wife was not within earshot, I posed this question: "Is your wife more attractive than the average woman?" The question invariably brought forth a blush, a smile, and laughter, as the subject recalled Garrison Keillor's famous benediction on *The Prairie Home Companion*: ". . . and that's the news from Lake Wobegone, where all the women are strong, all the men are goodlooking, and all the children are above average."

But I pursued the issue, and, after a prelude of blushing and stammering, every subject—to the last man—admitted that he, like the unskeptical masses, did indeed consider his wife more attractive than average. A similar experiment conducted in my home town of Louisville, Kentucky, among friends blessed with children, revealed that each and every one thought their kids more intelligent than average—for the majority, much more intelligent. Even those parents whose offspring scored toward the bottom of their class blamed this failing on a lack of motivation or on untalented teachers. In fact, I have yet to meet a man—myself included—who confesses to an ugly spouse or a stupid child. This irrational certainty, I would argue, is nothing more than the placebo effect with its white coat removed.

We live in a chimerical world, a world that allows a statistically impossible distribution of personal qualities. To survive, it seems, we must all believe in blatant falsehoods. In his innermost heart, no man considers himself an ordinary human, breeding and foraging for food and shelter on a planet as mortal and doomed as the creatures inhabiting it. Astronomers assure us that the universe will someday end in a Big Crunch or a Big Freeze, destroying all record of human existence, but we set about our lives each morning as though an eternity of fruitful days lie before us. Indeed, I could argue that we all live in Lake Wobegone, a psycho-spiritual community whose meaning and purpose, whose fragile, treasured affections, derive in large measure from the placebo effect.

We admire our scientists. We turn to them for the needs served only by the cold fires of reason, but the nonsense we preach to ourselves is cut from the same cloth—and every bit as precious—as the nonsense preached by CAM's shamans.

EVALUATING THE AUTHOR'S ARGUMENTS:

What do you think John Gamel was trying to accomplish with the anecdote that begins the viewpoint? What do you think Gamel's opinion of CAM is? Explain. Do you think alternative medicine and mainstream medicine have anything in common?

The National Center for Complementary and Alternative Medicine Provides Benefits to the American Public

"NCCAM will fulfill its obligation to the American public and health care providers to determine how, when, and under what circumstances CAM works."

Josephine P. Briggs and Richard J. Turman

In the following viewpoint Josephine P. Briggs and Richard J. Turman testify before a U.S. congressional committee about the work being done by the National Center for Complementary and Alternative Medicine (NCCAM). According to Briggs and Turman, a growing number of Americans are using complementary and alternative medicine (CAM) to improve and maintain their health. Thus, it is important that CAM is supported by sound science. Briggs and Turman point out the ways in which

Josephine P. Briggs and Richard J. Turman, "Witness Appearing Before the House Subcommittee on Labor-HHS-Education Appropriations," Fiscal Year 2009 Budget Report, March 5, 2008. Reproduced by permission of www.nccam.nih.gov.

NCCAM is fulfilling its obligation to the American public: It is helping to build a foundation of scientific evidence supporting CAM, it is improving CAM research, and it is training CAM researchers in scientific procedures. Josephine P. Briggs is the director of NCCAM, and Richard J. Turman is a deputy assistant secretary at the NCCAM.

AS YOU READ, CONSIDER THE FOLLOWING QUESTIONS:
1. According to Briggs and Turman, what two conventional medical organizations published new treatment guidelines for back pain that included acupuncture?
2. Briggs and Turman say that the more complex a CAM intervention is, the more difficult it is to do what?
3. What is the name of the educational program launched by NCCAM to educate physicians, other health-care providers, and patients about CAM?

The public's concept of health is broader than preventing and treating disease. Increasingly, Americans are using strategies that they can employ themselves to improve their health, maintain wellness, and improve quality of life. As part of this participatory approach to health, millions of people are using complementary and alternative medicine (CAM). Many of the leading U.S. medical institutions now offer integrative medicine services. These programs include personalized CAM interventions such as yoga, meditation, massage, and acupuncture. However, we know relatively little about the true potential of CAM to improve health and well being or to preempt disease, or about how best to use most CAM modalities. We also need to understand how CAM practices interact with other therapies and whether they are safe.

Given this consumer-driven call for better approaches to improved health and wellness, the medical research community has begun to explore promising CAM approaches and develop the scientific evidence base for CAM modalities that can be integrated as part of comprehensive health care. Using proven scientific methods and rigorous standards, NCCAM [the National Center for Complementary and Alternative Medicine] is building the research enterprise and the evidence base to better understand CAM. Through scientific investigation, research training programs, and outreach activities, NCCAM's efforts will support the rational integration of proven CAM approaches with conventional medicine.

Developing the Evidence Base of CAM

The scientific evidence base for integrative medicine will rest on data from both clinical trials and basic research that elucidates biological mechanisms. In 2007, NCCAM supported *The Status and Future of Acupuncture Research: 10 Years Post-NIH* [National Institutes of Health] *Consensus Conference,* which reviewed the current state of acupuncture research and charted future directions. This workshop showcased research on the effects of acupuncture and its clinical application for a number of health conditions, including pain control for osteoarthritis and back pain. It also highlighted advances in understanding the physiological processes involved in chronic pain and its response to acupuncture. Using state-of-the-art imaging technology, investigators found differences in the responses to acupuncture between healthy individuals and others with chronic pain from carpal tunnel syndrome. These differences point to the role of specific neurobiological pathways in the response to acupuncture, and to more effective approaches for the management of chronic pain. There is increasing acceptance of acupuncture by conventional medicine: the American Pain Society and the American College of Physicians have published new clinical treatment guidelines for persistent back pain that include acupuncture as a treatment option.

Increasingly, the successful paradigm employed by NCCAM in supporting rigorous basic, preclinical, and clinical research on acupuncture is being extended to other CAM modalities. Guided by its strategic plan, *Expanding Horizons of Health Care,* NCCAM's research agenda balances support for a broad range of investigator-initiated basic, translational, and clinical research with targeted initiatives to fill gaps in the CAM knowledge base. . . .

Improving the Conduct of CAM Research

There are special challenges inherent in the conduct of rigorous CAM research. Experience has taught us that basic and non-clinical CAM research, including mechanistic, dose-ranging, pharmacokinetic [the process by which a drug works in the body], and bioavailability studies, are essential building blocks in designing successful clinical trials that can yield clear results concerning the efficacy, optimal application, and safety of CAM interventions. NCCAM has incorporated these principles in its *Centers of Excellence for Research on CAM (CERC)* program. Three new CERCs will focus on basic and clinical research on compounds derived from plants for the prevention and treatment of chronic diseases. To better understand the composition, purity, and stability of biological products used in CAM research, NCCAM developed policies and review procedures to ensure that botanical and other materials used in clinical trials are research grade. Botanical and herbal medicine researchers regard the Center's policies as a "gold-standard" for ensuring the quality and reproducibility of research results.

Additional clinical research methods are needed to study the safety and efficacy of CAM practices. The Institute of Medicine concurs with this perspective. One particularly promising approach draws upon health services research methodology and resources to study effectiveness of CAM use. . . . It is important that CAM practices be tested in a manner that respects their integrity as they are practiced in the field. The more complex an intervention, the more difficult it

The National Center for Complementary and Alternative Medicine's research has found acupuncture to be a viable medical treatment.

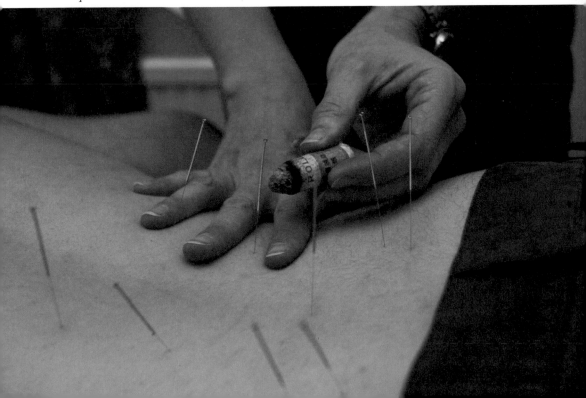

is to design a clinical trial of the therapy's benefits and risks. In the first of a series, NCCAM recently funded a workshop at Georgetown University that explored methods drawn from systems biology and complexity science for their potential in CAM. NCCAM's initiative, *Omics and Variable Responses to CAM: Secondary Analysis of CAM Clinical Trials,* will support genomics, proteomics, and metabolomics studies on the biological basis for differences in individual responses to CAM. Such innovative scientific tools and technology hold great promise in advancing predictive CAM research.

Training CAM Researchers and Facilitating Outreach

Rigorous basic, translational, and clinical CAM research cannot be accomplished without the sustained collaboration between CAM

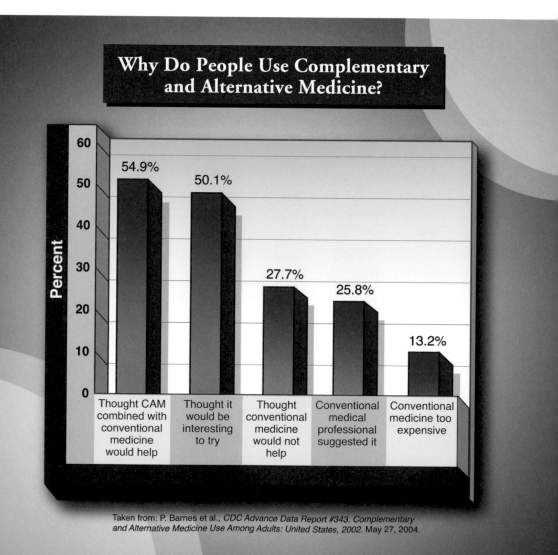

Why Do People Use Complementary and Alternative Medicine?

Taken from: P. Barnes et al., *CDC Advance Data Report #343. Complementary and Alternative Medicine Use Among Adults: United States, 2002.* May 27, 2004.

practitioners and experienced scientists. To increase CAM research capacity, NCCAM supports a variety of research training and career development programs as well as supplements for pre-doctoral and post-doctoral students, CAM practitioners, and conventional medical researchers and practitioners. In collaboration with the Bernard Osher Foundation and the Foundation for the National Institutes of Health, NCCAM will fund research career development awards that provide up to 5 years of clinical research career development to individuals holding CAM health professional doctoral degrees, including doctors of naturopathy, chiropractic, and acupuncture and oriental medicine. This is the first NIH training program that is expressly for CAM practitioners.

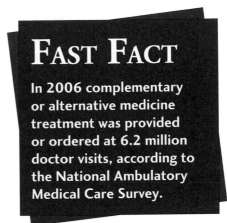

FAST FACT

In 2006 complementary or alternative medicine treatment was provided or ordered at 6.2 million doctor visits, according to the National Ambulatory Medical Care Survey.

NCCAM continues as the leading source of authoritative scientific information on CAM, both for the public and health care professionals. Participatory health care depends on an open and respectful dialogue between patients and their health care providers. Numerous studies have documented that a dialogue on CAM use is frequently lacking. To help address this problem, in 2007, NCCAM launched a new educational campaign, *Time to Talk*. The program provides physicians and other health providers and their patients with a range of educational materials aimed at ensuring that providers know the full extent of CAM being used by patients, and that an environment is created in which this information can be shared and discussed openly. . . .

NCCAM is also directing communication efforts toward students in training for careers in medicine, dentistry, nursing, and allied health professions. NCCAM funded 15 education project grants that incorporated basic CAM health education information into established curricula and continuing education programs. These projects were highlighted in the October 2007 issue of *Academic Medicine,* the journal of the Association of American Medical Colleges.

Heading Forward

It is clear that CAM research is an evolving scientific enterprise requiring collaboration across many scientific, medical, and CAM disciplines. More must be done to develop the capacity to conduct basic, translational, and clinical CAM research that incorporates state-of-the-art scientific methods and respects fundamental tenets of CAM practice. . . . As the new Director of NCCAM, I [Josephine P. Briggs] am looking forward to building new collaborations among the CAM and medical research communities, CAM practitioners, and other constituencies that will expand the potential of CAM to prevent and treat disease and to improve people's quality of life. Through these and other activities, NCCAM will fulfill its obligation to the American public and health care providers to determine how, when, and under what circumstances CAM Works.

EVALUATING THE AUTHORS' ARGUMENTS:

Josephine P. Briggs and Richard J. Turman say that NCCAM is helping to determine how, when, and under what circumstances CAM works. By doing this, they say they are fulfilling their obligation to the American public. Why do you think these determinations about CAM are benefiting the American public?

The National Center for Complementary and Alternative Medicine Should Be Eliminated

Wallace Sampson

"NCCAM could be dissolved, its functions returned to other [National Institutes of Health] centers, with no loss of knowledge, and an economic gain."

In the following viewpoint Wallace Sampson argues that the National Center for Complementary and Alternative Medicine (NCCAM) should be eliminated. Sampson says that the agency is *supposed* to conduct scientific studies on the claims of complementary and alternative medicine (CAM). However, in reality, the agency promotes CAM and lends legitimacy to treatments that Sampson believes are false. Sampson argues that nothing would be lost if the NCCAM were eliminated. However, there would be much to gain, such as all the money currently being used to "study" these foolish methods. Sampson is the editor of the *Scientific Review of Alternative Medicine* and emeritus

Wallace Sampson, "The Alternative Universe," *Quackfiles.com*, March 11, 2005. Reproduced by permission.

clinical professor of medicine at Stanford University, where he teaches analysis of unfounded medical claims. The data in the following article is as of 2005.

AS YOU READ, CONSIDER THE FOLLOWING QUESTIONS:
1. According to Sampson, the NCCAM seems to be tolerated for three reasons. What are these reasons?
2. What U.S. senator does Sampson say established the Office of Alternative Medicine (OAM), which was the first incarnation of NCCAM?
3. How much money does Sampson say the NCCAM awarded for psychic healing?

It is time for Congress to defund the National Center for Complementary and Alternative Medicine (NCCAM). After ten years of existence and over $200 million in expenditures, it has not proved effectiveness for any "alternative" method. It has added to proof of ineffectiveness of some methods, but we had that disproof before NCCAM was formed. . . . Its major accomplishment has been to ensure the positions of school faculty who might become otherwise employed—in more productive pursuits.

Such situations are not often tolerated in scientific fields—at least attempts are made to minimize them. NCCAM seems to be tolerated for three reasons. First, economically strapped medical schools welcome the funds. Second, although most medical scientists recognize the scientific absurdity of most "alternative" claims, most grant recipients and a few deans harbor the same absurd beliefs as do the advocates about the methods' efficacy. Third, and most important, major congressional powers are "CAM" advocates. They have a tight hold on the NIH [National Institutes of Health] budgets that fund investigations of real medical science as well. The deal seems to be that if the schools will play ball with and not oppose the senators, the senators will be generous in kind.

Classical Quackery and a Powerful Senator
While the public is distracted by terror attacks, wars, and personal and business scandals, modern medicine's integrity is being eroded by New

Age mysticism, cult-like schemes, ideologies, and classical quackery, all known as "alternative medicine." Using obscure language and misleading claims, they promote changes that would propel medicine back five centuries or more. They would supplant objectivity and reason with myths, feelings, hunches and sophistry. NCCAM is being presented as a scientific vehicle to study alternative medicine's anomalous methods. But NCCAM actually promotes the movement by assuming that false and implausible claims are legitimate things to study.

In 1992, Senator Tom Harkin, convinced that his allergies were cured by bee pollen, assigned $2 million of his discretionary funds to establish the Office of Alternative Medicine (OAM)—NCCAM's first incarnation. OAM was assigned to investigate the "alternative" methods that medical science considered false or implausible. But since their inception, OAM and NCCAM have had serious problems.

Problems at the Agency

The first OAM director resigned under Sen. Harkin's pressure, having objected to Harkin's OAM Council nominees who represented cancer scams such as the Laetrile and Tijuana cancer clinics. One influential Harkin collaborator and constituent was a travel agent for a Bahamas cancer clinic. And The Federal Trade Commission fined Harkin's bee pollen distributor, $200,000 for false claims.

In 1998, Dr. Edward Halperin, President of the North Carolina Medical Association called for disbanding the Office. Responding to objections from the science and medicine communities, NIH Director Harold Varmus placed OAM under more scientific NIH control. But Sen. Harkin countered, elevating OAM to an independent Center. By 2001, the annual budget rocketed to nearly $90 million per year and by 2002, over $100 million per year. Congress, believing erroneously that public demand for unscientific services had increased, passed appropriations without a dissenting vote.

Scientists look at the facts. They see that no sectarian or aberrant method has cured a single person, or extended a life for as much as a day. They see the "CAM" movement to be responding to people's irrational reactions to illness and narcissistic, self-centered wishes. They see no chance for "alternative" or "complementary" methods to replace modern methods. Recent surveys show that the methods merely add on to scientific medicine—adding to cost of care.

Senator Tom Harkin is given credit for establishing the Office of Alternative Medicine (OAM) in 1992. The author thinks its successor, NCCAM, should be discontinued.

We already know that these aberrant methods do not work, or are so unlikely to work that more clinical trials are not reasonable. Why is that? Because we have found the best quality studies are uniformly negative. Most positive studies are poorly designed and poorly controlled.

Hundreds of Years, Hundreds of Tests, and Still No Proof

Looking at the most popularly promoted methods we find that acupuncture, after thirty years, over 400 clinical trials, and 33 comprehensive literature reviews of those trials, only two specific conditions were found affected by acupuncture more than sham procedures. But even those effects are minimal, they are not superior to standard medical methods, they remain implausible and unpredictable. They will probably not be confirmed because their results are best explained by biased experimental errors.

After 100 years and hundreds of trials, chiropractic manipulation shows no advantage over shams for any condition. As for homeopathy, after 200 years and hundreds of studies, researchers cannot prove an effect for any homeopathic remedy for any condition. After a dozen studies, prolonged survival from psychological support for cancer patients has been essentially disproved. Herb product contents cannot be controlled, and their contents have been proved harmful. Some products have been adulterated with common pharmaceutical drugs that account for their apparent effects. If supplement marketers were held responsible for product effects, what more would there be to research?. . .

Throwing Money Away

But what is the NCCAM record? After eight years of projects and over $200 million, NCCAM and advocates have not proved any method to be effective. Perhaps more important, NCCAM has not declared any method to be ineffective, thus keeping open continuing congressional appropriations.

NCCAM is ridden with potential and actual conflicts of interest. Ten individuals account for 20% of NCCAM awards. None of them has produced a definitively positive or negative report. Most recipients have produced no report at all. Two individuals originally on the Advisory Council that approves NCCAM policy were awarded over $4 million and $5 million in repeated awards.

NCCAM recently announced research on "chelation therapy" for heart disease—a method

> **FAST FACT**
>
> The National Center for Complementary and Alternative Medicine received a budget of $121.6 million for fiscal year 2008.

already disproved and potentially dangerous. And $10 million is planned for research into herbs with their uncontrollable contents

"Snap out of it."

and unreliable results. Similarly troubling is NCCAM's awards of over $1 million into psychic healing, and $1.5 million for homeopathy. Both are highly implausible, being not only repeated failures, but promoted falsely as well.

NCCAM recently awarded $15 million to nine medical schools to develop teaching of these subjects—all by advocates of "CAM." It gave no funds to the five medical school courses with curricula already developed that teach about the subject rationally. In other words, NCCAM's research agenda fits its congressional supporters' ideological vision and finds unproductive ways to use up its ballooning appropriations. . . .

Rigorous trials cost $1–5 million each. Five to twenty trials are needed to prove or disprove effectiveness of each product or method. After staff expenses, $100 million per year can support only 10–20 reliable trials per year. Given hundreds of products and methods for hundreds of conditions, costs would be hundreds of billions to trillions of dollars over decades—all to prove what we already know. Then, as occurred after the negative Laetrile and vitamin C trials for cancer, advocates just think up new claims, or claim that the trials were rigged. Sales continue regardless of the disproof. By finding them worthy of study, NCCAM lends legitimacy to implausible methods, resulting in the public spending tens of billions of dollars annually on them.

Foolish and Unwise Policy

We also know that ill-conceived research produces misleading results. The results then lead to repetitive cycles of unproductive work to explain what was found, usually just to disprove the erroneous results. As a result of all this, claims continue.

Tens of millions of U.S. citizens lack medical insurance. Millions of illegal residents produce economic burdens on local medical systems. While real medicine and technology solve these problems and prolong productive life, "alternatives" appeal mostly to disaffected health dilettantes, and add nothing to public health. Worse, CAM's fuzzy thinking style and radical social ideology lead to wrong-headed policies such as the denial of HIV as the cause of AIDS, and the recent fears of vaccinations and electromagnetic fields.

Special commercial interests and irrational, wishful thinking created NCCAM. NCCAM is the only entity in the NIH devoted to an ideological approach to health. To correct the situation, Congress must consider at least interrupting funding of NCCAM while results of work in progress mature. NCCAM could be dissolved, its functions returned to other NIH centers, with no loss of knowledge, and an economic gain. Funds could be invested into studies of how such misadventures into "alternative" medicine can be avoided, and on studying the warping of human perceptions and beliefs that led to the present situation. More public money for investigating methods with negligible promise is foolish economics and even more, is unwise public policy.

EVALUATING THE AUTHOR'S ARGUMENTS:

What do you think Wallace Sampson believes is the mission of the National Center for Complementary and Alternative Medicine (NCCAM)? Is this the same obligation to the American public that was referred to in the previous viewpoint? What evidence does Sampson use to support his contention that the NCCAM is not fulfilling its mission?

Many U.S. Medical Schools Are Teaching Alternative Medicine

Katherine S. Mangan

"Students who are flocking to courses in alternative medicine are looking for more than a way to protect their patients from harm."

In the following viewpoint Katherine S. Mangan says that more and more medical schools are incorporating alternative medicine into their curricula. Mangan says that the University of Pennsylvania (Penn) School of Medicine, the nation's oldest medical school, combines conventional classes on things such as antibodies and surgery with classes that teach about acupuncture, herbs, and other alternative medicine treatments. According to Mangan, medical students are clamoring to get into the alternative medicine classes. Despite some opposition, according to Mangan, more and more medical schools are joining Penn and teaching alternative medicine practices. Katherine S. Mangan is a national correspondent for the *Chronicle of Higher Education.*

Robert M. Duggan cradles the wrist of a second-year student at the University of Pennsylvania [Penn] School of Medicine while another acupuncturist demonstrates how she would insert a stainless-steel needle into the student's scalp to relieve lower-back pain or lessen a migraine.

Sixteen medical students sit cross-legged on the floor, in rapt attention. "If someone puts a needle in the proper place, I feel an immediate response in the pulse," Mr. Duggan explains. "It's like a light switch turning on."

The students, many of them groggy from late nights of studying and hours of hospital rotations, discuss the ways in which the body, mind, and emotions are connected. Marc Hoffmann, another second-year student, recounts how a persistent lump in his throat disappeared after he broke down from pent-up frustration and sadness.

Mr. Duggan's explanation—that the cathartic release of his crying relaxed his muscles and dislodged a blockage of qi, or life energy—makes sense to him. "Maybe not as a medical student, but as a person," Mr. Hoffmann says.

Alternative Medicine at the Nation's Oldest Medical School

Lessons like these are taking place every week at Penn, the nation's oldest medical school, where students can now learn about acupuncture, herbs, and meditation along with antibiotics, surgery, and other staples of conventional Western medicine.

The Association of American Medical Colleges reports that at least 97 of the nation's 125 accredited medical schools cover alternative or complementary medicine in at least one required course, and that the number has been growing steadily since the early 1990s. In addition, 65 medical schools offer optional courses and seminars like the overview of alternative medicine being taught by Mr. Duggan, president of the Tai Sophia Institute for the Healing Arts, a graduate school of complementary medicine in Laurel, Md. At times, they do so over the objections of a small number of faculty members who view alternative therapies as flaky, or even dangerous.

"All we're doing is educating students about an area that their patients are increasingly turning to," says Alfred P. Fishman, a professor of medicine at Penn and director of the medical school's Office of Complementary and Alternative Therapies. "We think it would be a mistake not to prepare our students to critically evaluate what they're seeing." He points out that Penn is not teaching students how to perform alternative therapies, but simply to better understand how they work.

Controversial Collaboration

Earlier this year [2005] Penn's medical school announced that it had signed an affiliation agreement with Tai Sophia to collaborate on education and research.

The partnership raised eyebrows, and a few hackles, when *The Philadelphia Inquirer* published a front-page article in May [2005] describing the agreement. The plan called for the creation of a master's degree in complementary and alternative medicine, to be offered by Tai Sophia but available to Penn's medical and nursing students. Alternative medicine would also be integrated into traditional cardiac care.

The backlash, while limited to a handful of faculty members and alumni, was swift.

"Once that article appeared, the word spread like wildfire," says Gail Morrison, vice dean for education at the medical school. "We heard from alumni and faculty saying, 'What are you doing? What's happening to Penn?'" Some alums, she says, "thought we had lost our marbles."

Robert L. Park, a professor of physics at the University of Maryland at College Park and a frequent critic of alternative medicine, described the partnership in a blog with the headline: "Voodoo Medicine: Tai Sophia and Penn Med Form a Partnership." In it, he accused the medical school of "pandering to the public's obsession with mystic healing." A later posting claimed the medical school had "quietly severed ties to Tai Sophia."

For weeks, medical-school administrators did not return telephone calls or e-mail messages asking about the affiliation they had trumpeted in a news release months before. When they finally did, they explained that the agreement should have been described more loosely as a partnership, not an affiliation. Tai Sophia has been consulting with faculty members from Penn as it moves forward with plans for the master's-degree program.

"It was never meant to be a joining of the two schools," Dr. Morrison says. The goal is to educate students about forms of treatment that more than one-third of Americans turn to, according to the latest survey from the National Center for Complementary and Alternative Medicine, established in 1998 as part of the National Institutes of Health [NIH]. That figure includes practices that are considered mainstream, like following a special diet such as the Atkins plan, practicing yoga, or getting a massage.

Dr. Morrison says physicians should know, for example, if an herbal remedy a patient is using might interfere with his chemotherapy. "The public wants to use it and looks to you for information and advice," she says. "If you have no idea what it is or how it could potentially cause a problem, you're not being a very good physician."

What Alternative Medicine Can Offer

But students who are flocking to courses in alternative medicine are looking for more than a way to protect their patients from harm. Many see no reason why they should not refer a patient to a chiropractor or acupuncturist if other methods have failed.

"It's vital that we establish some kind of link between these systems," says Mr. Hoffmann, the Penn student. "Our system is really great if someone gets hit by a truck—no one runs off to an herbalist in that case—but there are a lot of chronic diseases for which we don't have good therapies, like arthritis and lupus," which might respond to herbs or yoga.

Learning techniques like meditation and deep breathing can also help medical students and health-care workers reduce their own stress, says Michael J. Baime, a clinical assistant professor of internal medicine and director of the Penn Program for Stress Management.

Doctors, nurses, and other health-care workers take time out to meditate on the cardiac floor of a Penn teaching hospital—an exercise that not only relieves tension, but also helps them work together more effectively, Dr. Baime explains in his office, which is decorated with a small Buddhist shrine, candles, and richly colored tapestries.

Health-care workers who are calm and "centered" listen better to patients, even when they have only a few minutes to spend with them, he says. "Every time you approach a patient's room, stop for three breaths before you open the door," Dr. Baime tells students in a class on meditation. "It's not anything magic or esoteric."

"The ultimate goal," he says, "is to create a connection between caregiver and patient that lets the patient know there's a real person there who's not just caring for an amalgam of organs, but a complex person with emotions and feelings."

Today, more medical schools are offering courses in alternative medicine.

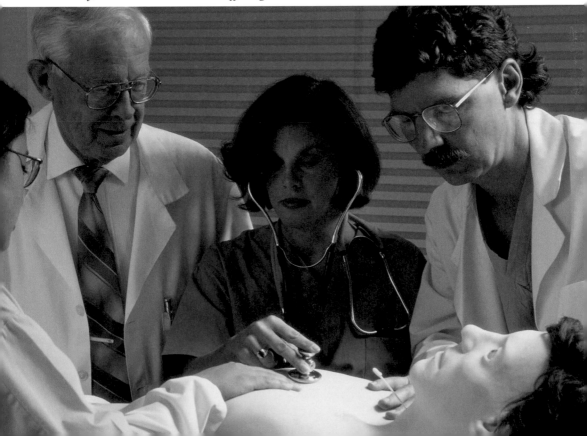

Fear of the Unknown

Nontraditional methods are making inroads at other medical schools, as well. Pamela Gandy, a staff acupuncturist at the University of Maryland Health Center, has helped acupuncturists set up services in college health centers around the country, including those at the University of Massachusetts at Amherst and Towson University.

Working alongside traditional medical doctors at Maryland's health center, where acupuncture is covered by students' health plans, Ms. Gandy helps educate doctors about her methods. She recalls the day one of her patients arrived with serious burns on her arm from accidentally leaning on her car radiator. With the patient's permission, Ms. Gandy inserted a needle into the woman's foot, near her smallest toe, and the woman said the burning sensation in her arm stopped.

"A lot of the skepticism is just fear of the unknown," Ms. Gandy says. "Even if they don't refer all of their patients to acupuncturists, at least they know what it's about." Alternative medicine, she adds, "is not mutually exclusive with Western medicine."

Hogwash, says Carl E. Bartecchi, one of the Penn medical alumni who wrote in to complain about the Penn–Tai Sophia partnership. Dr. Bartecchi, a specialist in internal medicine and clinical professor of medicine at the University of Colorado, wrote a 2003 book called *The Alternative Medicine Hoax*. He insists that Penn has distanced itself from Tai Sophia because of the opposition.

> ### FAST FACT
>
> According to the National Center for Complementary and Alternative Medicine, an estimated one-third of certified acupuncturists in the United States are medical doctors.

"At every medical school, there's a small group of alternative-medicine enthusiasts who push these things under the radar," he says. "When the real scientists learn what they're doing, they get rid of it."

Mainstream medical schools legitimize questionable alternative techniques when they integrate them into their curricula or practices, he argues. "Harvard is doing homeopathy in its hospitals, and when you ask why they're doing it, they say, 'We're conducting the

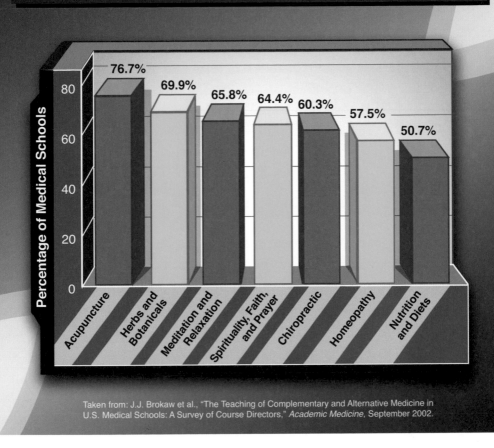

Percentage of U.S. Medical Schools Teaching Various Complementary and Alternative Medicine Subjects

76.7% Acupuncture
69.9% Herbs and Botanicals
65.8% Meditation and Relaxation
64.4% Spirituality, Faith, and Prayer
60.3% Chiropractic
57.5% Homeopathy
50.7% Nutrition and Diets

Percentage of Medical Schools: 80, 60, 40, 20, 0

Taken from: J.J. Brokaw et al., "The Teaching of Complementary and Alternative Medicine in U.S. Medical Schools: A Survey of Course Directors," *Academic Medicine*, September 2002.

research,'" he says. "But the organizations that are funding it are saying, 'It's offered at Harvard, so it must be valid.'"

He agrees that medical schools should teach about alternative medicine, and suggests his book as required reading: "Physicians need to be comfortable explaining the placebo effect, why some treatments are dangerous, why most are not worth the money, and why, by supporting such nonsense, you are only encouraging those therapists who are profiting from the lack of the patients' knowledge of their problem and potential treatments."

Thomas J. Wheeler, an associate professor of biochemistry and molecular biology at the University of Louisville School of Medicine, teaches an elective course, "A Scientific Look at Alternative Medicine," that encourages students to take a critical look at practitioners' claims.

While some techniques, like relaxation methods and the use of certain dietary supplements, make sense, "I'm a skeptic when it comes to most kinds of alternative medicine, he says. He argues that most medical-school courses on the topic lack scientific rigor, and that "dilutes the quality of medical education."

An administrator with the Association of American Medical Colleges says many medical professors are uncomfortable teaching about techniques that don't lend themselves to rigorous scientific analysis. "The resistance comes when you cross the line between teaching about alternative medicine and teaching students to use it," says Linda Lesky, assistant vice president for medical education.

Integrating Conventional and Alternative Medicine

The University of Arizona College of Medicine's integrative-medicine program comes closer than most to doing that. Led by the renowned author and physician Andrew Weil, the fellowship program teaches physicians how to perform techniques such as guided imagery, homeopathy, and osteopathic manipulation.

The program also offers electives to medical students, as well as a rotation in alternative medicine. Although the program attracted its share of controversy when it started in 1997, it is considered one of the leading programs integrating traditional and nontraditional medicine.

And at the Georgetown University School of Medicine, alternative medicine, including herbs, acupuncture, and massage, has been integrated throughout required courses as part of a $1.7-million NIH study. The university also offers a master's degree in physiology with a concentration in complementary and alternative medicine, taught by medical professors.

Students from a nearby massage school study anatomy at Georgetown, while its medical students learn about massage from the massage school.

"Our approach has been not one of advocacy but one of open-minded skepticism," says Aviad Haramati, a professor of physiology and biophysics who is the lead investigator on the NIH study. "As physicians, we need to know more about the safety and efficacy of the alternative methods our patients are using, and the only way to do that is by becoming partners."

And if, in the process, students learn new techniques for managing stress and communicating with their patients, it may be just what the doctor ordered.

EVALUATING THE AUTHOR'S ARGUMENTS:

Katherine S. Mangan asserts that U.S medical schools can provide benefits to patients and future physicians by teaching medical students about complementary and alternative medicine. She uses an ample number of quotations to support her viewpoint. Do you think she uses these quotations effectively? Do you think Mangan's viewpoint is subtle or obvious? Explain.

Viewpoint 6

U.S. Medical Schools Should Not Teach Alternative Medicine

Robert W. Donnell

"Our medical schools are devolving into Hogwarts-like institutions of eclectic healing arts."

In the following viewpoint Robert W. Donnell contends that medical schools should not teach alternative medicine. According to Donnell, alternative medicine is not rooted in science, and teaching it at our medical schools goes against everything that medicine has represented for almost one hundred years. Donnell says that early in the twentieth century, dogma and unscientific teaching were rampant in American medical education. This all changed after the publication of the Flexner Report, which put medical education on its correct track, according to Donnell: teaching only those things that are supported by science and reason. According to Donnell, medical schools that are combining homeopathy, ayurvedic medicine, or other alternative medicines with conventional medicine are moving medical education back to the

Robert W. Donnell, MD; Nicholas Genes, MD, PhD; and Roy M. Poses, MD, "Should Medical Schools Teach 'Integrative Medicine?'" *Medscape.com,* December 6, 2007. Copyright © 2007 by Medscape. Reproduced by permission. www.medscape.com/viewarticle/565472.

Dark Ages. Donnell is a physician at the Department of Medicine, St. Mary's Hospital in Rogers, Arkansas.

AS YOU READ, CONSIDER THE FOLLOWING QUESTIONS:
1. According to Donnell, who requested and who commissioned the Flexner Report?
2. What things does Donnell say doctors do need to know about alternative medicine treatments?
3. Donnell says that combining alternative medicine healing traditions with scientific methods is wrong because it leaves medicine without what?

A century ago, medical education lacked standardization and scientific discipline. To address the problem, the American Medical Association formed the Council on Medical Education (CME), tasked with restructuring the curricula of American medical schools. At the CME's request, the Carnegie Foundation commissioned Abraham Flexner to survey and report on the quality of medical schools in the United States and Canada. The Flexner Report that followed in 1910 was severely critical of medical education. In its aftermath, many medical schools closed or merged. Those that survived instituted major reforms.

The Flexner Report was revolutionary and even today is widely celebrated as a defining document for medical education. However, the last decade has seen a disturbing trend away from Flexner's warnings. Medical schools are reverting to pre-Flexnerian standards by adding pseudoscientific health claims to their course materials under the rubric of "integrative medicine."

Flexner condemned such claims, writing in Chapter X of the Report that they should have no place in medical education. Modern medicine, he said, "wants not dogma, but facts. It countenances no presupposition that is not

> **FAST FACT**
>
> In 2007 there were 70,225 students enrolled in U.S. medical schools, according to the Association of American Medical Colleges.

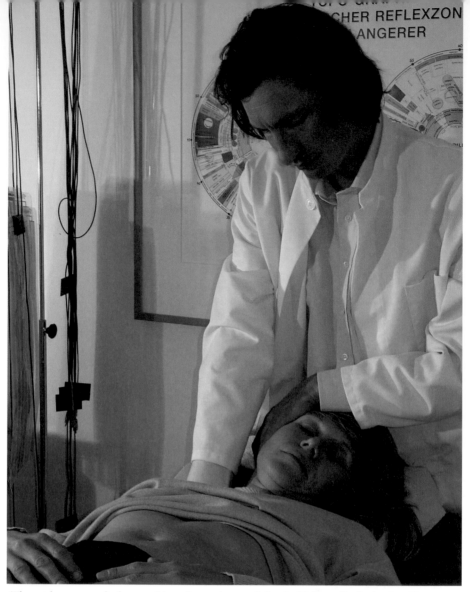

The author contends that teaching alternative medicine in U.S. medical schools will move medical education back to the Dark Ages.

common to it with all the natural sciences, with all logical thinking." Unfortunately, medical schools today not only countenance but teach and promote such presuppositions, many of which would require us to abandon basic science textbooks.

Let's make a distinction. Doctors need to know about the alternative treatments that patients are seeking so that they can recognize herb-drug interactions, engage patients in discussions about alternative treatments, and appreciate cultural differences that may lead patients to seek such treatments. Medical schools should equip students in these areas. However, they should teach an appropriately critical and scientific view of alternative theories.

For many medical schools today, that's the rub. Academic leaders, in fact, are suggesting that alternative modalities should be presented "in the context of their own philosophies and models of health and illness. Survey data from both MD- and DO [doctor of osteopathy]-granting schools confirm this trend. In other words, dubious claims are being promoted to students in an unscientific, uncritical manner. If you need more evidence, browse the Web sites of academic medical centers to see what's going on and note their promotions of therapeutic touch, homeopathy, Ayurvedic medicine, shamanism, chakras, and more.

So, you may say, what's wrong with combining other healing traditions with scientific methods? Plenty, because it results in an eclectic

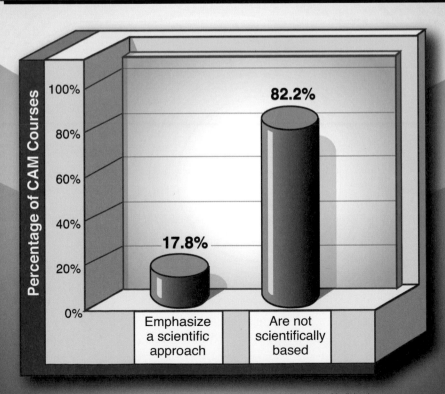

Few Complementary and Alternative Medicine Courses at U.S. Medical Schools Are Science Based

Percentage of CAM Courses

82.2%

17.8%

Emphasize a scientific approach

Are not scientifically based

Taken from: J.J. Brokaw et al., "The Teaching of Complementary and Alternative Medicine in U.S. Medical Schools: A Survey of Course Directors," *Academic Medicine*, September 2002.

mix of diverse theories with no common basis. It leaves medicine without a consistent scientific framework upon which to evaluate treatments.

The Flexner Report came down strongly against integrative medicine. In Chapter X, Flexner posed this question about the compatibility of scientific medicine with pseudoscientific claims, which he termed *dogma*: "Is it essential that we should now conclude a treaty of peace, by which the reduced number of medical schools should be pro-rated as to recognize dissenters on an equitable basis?" His emphatic answer was "no." He later continued: "The ebbing vitality of homeopathic schools is a striking demonstration of the incompatibility of science and dogma."

Unfortunately, academic medicine is now turning its back on Flexner's mandate. Our medical schools are devolving into Hogwarts-like [from the Harry Potter fantasy novel series] institutions of eclectic healing arts. Reforms are urgently needed so that medical education will once again be rooted in science.

EVALUATING THE AUTHORS' ARGUMENTS:

Do you think Robert W. Donnell disagrees with any teaching of complementary and alternative medicine (CAM) in U.S. medical schools? Or do you think he disagrees with the way CAM is being taught at U.S. medical schools? Explain. After reading this and the previous viewpoint, can you think of any points the authors might agree on?

Facts About Complementary and Alternative Medicine (CAM)

Editor's note: These facts can be used in reports or papers to reinforce or add credibility when making important points or claims.

According to the 2002 National Health Interview Survey, the ten most commonly used CAM therapies during the previous twelve months were:
- Use of prayer specifically for one's own health (43 percent);
- Prayer by others for one's own health (24 percent);
- Natural products (19 percent);
- Deep breathing exercises (12 percent);
- Participation in prayer group for one's own health (10 percent);
- Meditation (8 percent);
- Chiropractic care (7.5 percent);
- Yoga (5 percent);
- Massage (5 percent);
- Diet-based therapies (3.5 percent).

Facts About Why People Use CAM
According to the 2002 National Health Interview Survey:
- Fifty-five percent of adults said they were most likely to use CAM because they believed that it would help them when combined with conventional medical treatments.
- Fifty percent thought CAM would be interesting to try.
- Twenty-six percent used CAM because a conventional medical professional suggested they try it.
- Thirteen percent used CAM because they felt that conventional medicine was too expensive.
- CAM was most often used to treat back pain or other back problems, head or chest colds, neck pain or problems, joint pain or stiffness, and anxiety or depression.

Facts About Those Who Use CAM
According to the 2002 National Health Interview Survey:
- Women are more likely than men to use CAM.

- Older adults are more likely than younger adults to use CAM (including prayer in the definition of CAM).
- Middle-aged adults are more likely than both older and younger adults to use CAM (not including prayer).
- Black adults (68 percent) are more likely to use mind-body therapies than white adults (50 percent) or Asian adults (48 percent).
- Asian adults are more likely (43 percent) to use CAM than white adults (36 percent) or black adults (26 percent) (not including prayer and megavitamin therapy).
- White adults (12 percent) are more likely to use manipulative and body-based therapies than Asian adults (7 percent) or black adults (4 percent).
- Adults with higher levels of education are more likely to use CAM than those with lower levels of education (not including prayer).
- More affluent adults are more likely than poor adults to use CAM (not including prayer and megavitamin therapy).
- Poor adults are more likely than more affluent adults to use megavitamin therapy and prayer.
- Adults who live in urban areas are more likely than adults who live in rural areas to use alternative medical systems, biologically based therapies, and mind-body therapies.
- Former smokers are more likely to use CAM than current smokers or those who have never smoked.

Facts About Spending on CAM
According to National Health Surveys conducted in 1997:
- The U.S. public spent an estimated $36 billion to $47 billion on CAM therapies in 1997.
- Of this amount, between $12 billion and $20 billion was paid out of pocket for the services of professional CAM health-care providers.
- These fees represent more than the public paid out of pocket for all hospitalizations in 1997 and about half of what it paid for all out-of-pocket physician services.
- $5 billion of out-of-pocket spending was on herbal products.

According to a 2005 survey cited by *About.com*:
- Fourteen out of eighteen major health maintenance organizations and insurance providers, including Aetna, Medicare, Prudential,

and Kaiser Permanente, covered at least eleven of thirty-four alternative therapies.
- Chiropractic, massage therapy, and acupuncture are the three most-covered therapies, followed by naturopathic medicine.

Facts About CAM and Cancer

According to the National Cancer Institute, people with cancer may use CAM to:
- help cope with the side effects of cancer treatments, such as nausea, pain, and fatigue;
- comfort themselves and ease the worries of cancer treatment and related stress;
- feel that they are doing something more to help with their own care;
- try to treat or cure their cancer.

The National Center for Complementary and Alternative Medicine has sponsored the following clinical trials to study CAM and cancer:
- Acupuncture to relieve neck and shoulder pain following surgery for head or neck cancer.
- Ginger as a treatment for nausea and vomiting caused by chemotherapy.
- Massage for the treatment of cancer pain.
- Mistletoe extract combined with chemotherapy for the treatment of solid tumors.

Organizations to Contact

The editors have compiled the following list of organizations concerned with the issues debated in this book. The descriptions are derived from materials provided by the organizations. All have publications or information available for interested readers. The list was compiled on the date of publication of the present volume; the information provided here may change. Be aware that many organizations take several weeks or longer to respond to queries, so allow as much time as possible.

The Alternative Medicine Foundation (AMF)
PO Box 60016
Potomac, MD 20859
(301) 340-1960
fax: (301) 340-1936
Web site: www.amfoundation.org

The Alternative Medicine Foundation is a nonprofit organization formed to respond to the public and professional need for responsible and reliable education, information, and dialogue about the integration of alternative and conventional medicine. The foundation works to conserve and respect the knowledge and practice of indigenous therapies and systems of health care, promote novel ways to blend ancient practice and modern science for the promotion of health, and advance the ethical and sustainable development of alternatives to standard care. The AMF provides several resource guides on its Web site.

American Association of Acupuncture and Oriental Medicine (AAAOM)
PO Box 162340
Sacramento, CA 95816
(916) 443-4770
fax: (916) 443-4766
Web site: www.aaaomonline.org

The American Association of Acupuncture and Oriental Medicine works to establish, maintain, and advance the professional field of

Oriental medicine, with acupuncture and other modalities, as a distinct, primary-care field of medicine. The organization also seeks to integrate acupuncture and Oriental medicine into mainstream health care in the United States and to educate policy makers, health-care workers, and the general public about Oriental medicine and acupuncture. The AAAOM publishes the *American Acupuncturist*, a professional acupuncture journal.

American Association of Cancer Research (AACR)
615 Chestnut St., 17th Floor
Philadelphia, PA 19106-4404
(215) 440-9300 or (866) 423-3965
fax: (215) 440-9313
e-mail: aacr@aacr.org
Web site: www.aacr.org

The American Association of Cancer Research is a nonprofit organization that seeks to prevent and cure cancer through research, education, and communication. Through its programs and services, the AACR fosters research in cancer and related biomedical science; accelerates the dissemination of new research findings among scientists and others dedicated to the conquest of cancer; promotes science education and training; and advances the understanding of cancer etiology, prevention, diagnosis, and treatment throughout the world. AACR publishes six peer-reviewed scientific journals: *Cancer Research; Clinical Cancer Research; Molecular Cancer Therapeutics; Molecular Cancer Research; Cancer Epidemiology, Biomarkers & Prevention;* and *Cancer Prevention Research.* The AACR also publishes *CR*, a magazine for cancer survivors and their families, patient advocates, physicians, and scientists.

American Chiropractic Association (ACA)
1701 Clarendon Blvd.
Arlington, VA 22209
(703) 276-8800
fax: (703) 243-2593
e-mail: memberinfo@acatoday.org
Web site: www.acatoday.org

The American Chiropractic Association is the largest professional association in the world representing doctors of chiropractic. The ACA provides lobbying, public relations, and professional and educational opportunities for doctors of chiropractic; funds research regarding chiropractic and health issues; and offers leadership for the advancement of chiropractic. The ACA offers several publications, including *American Chriopractic News* and the *Journal of the American Chiropractic Association.*

American College for Advancement in Medicine (ACAM)
24411 Ridge Route Dr., Suite 115
Laguna Hills, CA 92653
(949) 309-3520
fax: (949) 309-3538
e-mail: info@acam.org
Web site: www.acam.org

The American College for Advancement in Medicine is a nonprofit association dedicated to educating physicians and other health-care professionals on the latest findings and emerging procedures in complementary, alternative, and integrative (CAIM) medicine. The ACAM accomplishes its mission by funding medical research for treatments that will support and enhance complementary modalities and integrative therapies; providing assistance for public programs and group forums that champion patient rights through education, information, and access to CAIM therapies; and providing educational scholarship for medical students from accredited medical schools seeking to enhance their scope of study with programs and seminars in complementary, alternative, and integrative medicine. ACAM news and links to related trials and organizations are found on the Web site.

American Medical Association (AMA)
515 N. State St.
Chicago, IL 60610
(800) 621-8335
Web site: www.ama-assn.org

The American Medical Association is the voice of the American medical establishment. Founded in 1847, the AMA is the largest organization of physicians and medical students in the United States. The AMA's mission is to promote the art and science of medicine for the betterment of public health, to advance the interests of physicians and their patients, to promote public health, to lobby for legislation favorable to physicians and patients, and to raise money for medical education. The organization publishes *American Medical News* and the *Journal of the American Medical Association* (*JAMA*), which has the largest circulation of any weekly medical journal in the world.

American Music Therapy Association, Inc.
8455 Colesville Rd., Suite 1000
Silver Spring, MD 20910
(301) 589-3300
fax: (301) 589-5175
e-mail: info@musictherapy.org
Web site: www.musictherapy.org

The American Music Therapy Association is an organization of music therapists whose mission is to advance public awareness of the benefits of music therapy and increase access to quality music therapy services. The association publishes a number of journals, including the *Journal of Music Therapy*, *Music Therapy Perspectives*, and *Music Therapy Matters*.

Annie Appleseed Project
7319 Serrano Terrace
Delray Beach, FL 33446-2215
e-mail: annieappleseedpr@aol.com
Web site: http://annieappleseedproject.org

The Annie Appleseed Project, founded by cancer survivor Ann Fonfa, is an organization that provides information, education, advocacy, and awareness about complementary and alternative cancer treatments. The project collects, studies, and reports on promising alternative cancer research. It also organizes and attends conferences and seminars on alternative cancer therapies. The project's Web site provides information on various types of cancer, alternative cancer treatments, and links to other alternative cancer treatment sites.

Committee for Skeptical Inquiry (CSI)
PO Box 703
Amherst, NY 14226
(716) 636-1425
e-mail: info@csicop.org
Web site: www.csicop.org

The Committee for Skeptical Inquiry is a nonprofit scientific and educational organization that encourages the critical investigation of paranormal and fringe-science claims and disseminates factual information about such claims. The organization promotes science and scientific inquiry, critical thinking, science education, and the use of reason in examining important issues. CSI publishes the journal the *Skeptical Inquirer* and the newsletter *Skeptical Briefs*.

National Cancer Institute (NCI)
NCI Public Inquiries Office
6116 Executive Blvd., Room 3036A
Bethesda, MD 20892-8322
(800) 422-6237
Web site: http://ncipoet.org

The National Cancer Institute, a component of the National Institutes of Health, is the federal government's agency for cancer research and training. The NCI coordinates the National Cancer Program, which conducts and supports research, training, health information dissemination, and other programs with respect to the cause, diagnosis, prevention, and treatment of cancer, rehabilitation from cancer, and the continuing care of cancer patients and the families of cancer patients. The NCI Web site offers a multitude of publications on cancer research, cancer testing, cancer prevention, cancer treatment, and many other topics.

The National Center for Complementary and Alternative Medicine (NCCAM)
National Institutes of Health
9000 Rockville Pike
Bethesda, MD 20892
or NCCAM Clearinghouse
PO Box 7923
Gaithersburg, MD 20898
(888) 644-6226
fax: (866) 464-3616
e-mail: info@nccam.nih.gov
Web site: http://nccam.nih.gov

The National Center for Complementary and Alternative Medicine is one of twenty-seven institutes and centers that make up the National

Institutes of Health within the U.S. Department of Health and Human Services. NCCAM is dedicated to exploring complementary and alternative healing practices in the context of rigorous science. The agency trains complementary and alternative medicine (CAM) researchers and disseminates information to the public and professionals. The center provides timely and accurate information about CAM research through its Web site, an information clearinghouse, fact sheets, distinguished lecture series, and publication databases.

National Center for Homeopathy (NCH)
801 N. Fairfax St., Suite 306
Alexandria, VA 22314
(703) 548-7790
fax: (703) 548-7792
Web site: http://nationalcenterforhomeopathy.org

The National Center for Homeopathy is an open-membership organization whose mission is to promote health through homeopathy. The organization provides educational resources to homeopaths and strives to educate the public about homeopathy. The NCH publishes a bimonthly journal, *Homeopathy Today*, as well as an electronic newsletter and various other resources.

National Council Against Health Fraud (NCAHF)
119 Foster St.
Peabody, MA 01960
(978) 532-9383
e-mail: ncahf.office@verizon.net
Web site: www.ncahf.org

The National Council Against Health Fraud is a private, nonprofit, voluntary health agency that focuses on health misinformation, fraud, and quackery as public health problems. Its funding is derived primarily from membership dues and individual donations. NCAHF appoints task forces to conduct extensive investigations on such issues as acupuncture, chiropractic, dubious health-care credentials, broadcast media abuse, vitamin abuse, questionable addiction treatments, medical neglect of children, and cancer quackery. NCAHF publishes an online newsletter, the *Consumer Health Digest*.

For Further Reading

Books

Altshuler, Larry. *Balanced Healing: Combining Modern Medicine with Safe and Effective Alternative Therapies.* Gig Harbor, WA: Harbor, 2004. Presents a balanced approach to health care by providing nonbiased, ailment-specific information.

Badaracco, Claire Hoertz. *Prescribing Faith: Medicine, Media, and Religion in American Culture.* Waco, TX: Baylor University Press, 2007. Badaracco asserts that media, religion, and medicine have been intertwined throughout American history, often to the detriment of American health.

Bausell, R. Barker. *Snake Oil Science: The Truth About Complementary and Alternative Medicine.* New York: Oxford University Press, 2007. Bausell builds a rigorous case against complementary and alternative medicine (CAM). He provides a look at the history of CAM and analyzes studies purporting to support it.

Cuellar, Norma. *Conversations in Complementary and Alternative Medicine.* Sudbury, MA: Jones & Bartlett, 2006. Cuellar interviews leading experts in complementary and alternative medicine. They each provide important insight into their particular specialty and the history of CAM.

Duke Center for Integrative Medicine, Richard Liebowitz, and Linda Smith. *The Duke Encyclopedia of New Medicine: Conventional and Alternative Medicine for All Ages.* New York: Rodale, 2006. A comprehensive resource of information on integrative medicine, i.e., medical approaches that combine conventional and alternative practices.

Fitzgerald, Randall. *The Hundred-Year Lie: How Food and Medicine Are Destroying Your Health.* New York: Dutton, 2006. Utilizing a range of articles from science journals and government reports, along with interviews with scientists and environmentalists, Fitzgerald looks at synthetic chemicals—from artificial sweeteners to antidepressants—that are diminishing our health. The author believes naturally occurring foods and medicines are more effective than synthetics.

Foster, Steven, and Rebecca Johnson. *Desk Reference to Nature's Medicine.* Washington, DC: National Geographic Society, 2006. A reference book of medicinal plants, including their origins, histories, and medicinal uses. Botanical drawings and maps are provided for each plant.

Freeman, Lynda. *Mosby's Complementary and Alternative Medicine. A Research-Based Approach.* St. Louis, MO: Mosby, 2004. A research-based textbook offering clinically relevant coverage of complementary and alternative medicine.

Fulghum, Debra, Bruce Krieger, and Dolores Krieger. *Miracle Touch: A Complete Guide to Hands-On Therapies That Have the Amazing Ability to Heal.* New York: Three Rivers, 2003. The authors provide in-depth information about "therapeutic touch" therapies, including acupuncture, acupressure, massage, reflexology, and Reiki.

Guyol, Gracelyn. *Healing Depression and Bipolar Disorder Without Drugs.* New York: Walker, 2006. Guyol uses moving, real-life stories of people suffering from debilitating forms of depression and bipolar disorder who eschewed mainstream medicine and found relief and healing with natural remedies.

Harrington, Anne. *The Cure Within: A History of Mind-Body Medicine.* New York: Norton, 2008. Harrington uses case studies and stories of healings to show how deeply embedded the idea of positive mental health is in the quest for physical health, and she looks at the ways conventional medicine uses mind-body concepts.

Robins, Natalie. *Copeland's Cure: Homeopathy and the War Between Conventional and Alternative Medicine.* New York: Knopf, 2005. Robins tells the story of New York senator Royal Copeland who, in the early part of the twentieth century, fought for the acceptance of homeopathy by mainstream medicine. Copeland was responsible for the inclusion of homeopathic remedies in the federal Food, Drug, and Cosmetic Act of 1938.

Singh, Simon, and E. Ernst. *Trick or Treatment: The Undeniable Facts About Alternative Medicine.* New York: Norton, 2008. The authors provide a reasoned examination of the research on acupuncture, homeopathy, chiropractic, herbal medicine, and other alternative treatments.

Trudeau, Kevin. *Natural Cures "They" Don't Want You to Know About.* Elk Grove Village, IL: Alliance, 2007. Trudeau believes conventional drugs approved by the government and marketed by big business are being pushed on consumers, and he thinks these drugs are actually the cause of illness and disease.

Whorton, James. *Nature Cures: The History of Alternative Medicine in America.* New York: Oxford University Press, 2002. Whorton traces the origins and influences of unconventional healing movements in nineteenth- and twentieth-century America.

Periodicals

Alternative Therapies in Health and Medicine. "The White House Commission on Complementary and Alternative Medicine Policy and the Future of Healthcare," September/October 2004.

Comarow, Avery. "Embracing Alternative Care: Top Hospitals Put Unorthodox Therapies into Practice," *U.S. News & World Report,* January 21, 2008.

Cooper, Edwin. "eCAM: Early Harvest," *Evidence-Based Complementary and Alternative Medicine,* 2008.

Crute, Sheree. "The Best Medicine," *AARP Magazine,* March/April 2008. www.aarpmagazine.org/health/best-medicine.html.

Economist. "Trust Me, I've Got a License: Alternative Medicine," April 19, 2008.

Einhorn, Bruce, and Arlene Weintraub. "Stem Cell Refugees," *Business Week,* February 12, 2007.

Fisher, Barbara Loe. "Doctors of Scientism: No Cure for Autism," *Vaccine Awakening,* August 22, 2007. www.whale.to/vaccine/fisher 49.html.

Gordon, James S. "Connecting Mind, Body, and Beyond," *Alternative Therapies in Health & Medicine,* March/April 2006.

Greten, Henry. "What Is the Role of Chinese Medical Theory in Modern Scientific Research?" *Journal of Acupuncture and Tuina Science,* 2008.

Hsiao, An-Fu, et al. "Role of Religiosity and Spirituality in Complementary and Alternative Medicine Use Among Cancer Survivors in California," *Integrative Cancer Therapies*, 2008.

Hyodo, Ichinosuke. "How Should Oncologists Face Complementary and Alternative Medicine?" *Japanese Journal of Clinical Oncology*, 2008.

Irwin, Megan. "Alternative Medicine Saved Our Lives," *Prevention*, September 2007.

Kirby, David. "The Next Big Autism Bomb: Are 1 in 50 Kids Potentially at Risk?" *Huffington Post*, March 26, 2008. www.huffingtonpost .com/david-kirby/the-next-big-autism-bomb_b_93627.html.

Kozlowski, Kim. "More Travel Overseas for Stem Cell Therapy," *Detroit News*, November 29, 2007.

Lampe, Frank, and Suzanne Snyder. "Nicholas J. Gonzalez, MD: Seeking the Truth in the Fight Against Cancer," *Alternative Therapies*, January/February 2007. www.alternative-therapies.com/ at/web_pdfs/gonzalez.pdf.

Lee, Paul. "No Justification for the Existence of Chiropractic," *Quackfiles .com*, 2004. www.geocities.com/healthbase/chiro-illegitimate.html.

Nelson, Bryn. "Stem Cell Researchers Face Down Stem Cell Tourism," *Nature*, June 5, 2008. www.nature.com/stemcells/2008/ 0806/080605/full/stemcells.2008.89.html; jsessionid=07999F3C8F 01EDCE084B05172DF6DEC4.

Onion. "FDA Approves Sale of Prescription Placebo," September 17, 2003. www.theonion.com/content/node/39082.

Roberts, Tara. "So You Want to Go into Alternative Health Care?" *CosmoGirl!* March 2008.

Sewitch, Maida, Monica Cepoiu, and Monica Rigillo. "A Literature Review of Health Care Professional Attitudes Toward Complementary and Alternative Medicine," *Complementary Health Practice Review*, 2008.

USA Today Magazine. "Fad Treatments on the Rise," October 2007.

Vastag, Brian. "Injections of Hope: Doctors Promote Offshore Stem Cell Shots, but Some Patients Cry Foul," *Washington Post*, September 2, 2008.

Wang Ling-Ling. "Experience of Treatment of Depression by Acupuncture plus Medicine," *Journal of Acupuncture and Tuina Science*, 2008.

Weisman, Roanne. "Our Lives Were in Our Hands," *Prevention*, May 2008.

Wolman, David. "The Truth About Autism: Scientists Reconsider What They Think They Know," *Wired*, February 25, 2008. www.wired. com/medtech/health/magazine/16-03/ff_autism?currentPage=all.

Yun, Wu, Zhen Jin, and Ke Li. "Effect of Acupuncture on the Brain in Children with Spastic Cerebral Palsy Using Functional Neuroimaging," *Journal of Child Neurology*, 2008.

Web Sites

Bad Science (www.badscience.net). A Web site from Ben Goldacre, English doctor and author of the Bad Science column in the newspaper the *Guardian*.

Consumer Lab (www.consumerlab.com). A Web site that provides independent test results and information to help consumers and health-care professionals evaluate dietary supplements and herbs.

The Integrator Blog (http://theintegratorblog.com). A Web site offering news, opinions, reports, and networking for those who practice integrative and complementary medicine.

Mayo Clinic (www.mayoclinic.com/health/alternative-medicine/ CM99999). A Web site from the Mayo Clinic, an internationally known and respected health-care organization, which provides information on complementary and alternative medicine and therapies.

Natural News (www.naturalnews.com). An online source of information, articles, and commentary promoting natural and other alternative healing remedies.

Quackwatch (www.quackwatch.com). A comprehensive Web site providing hundreds of links to articles and sites that shed light on alternative medicine claims.

Index

A

Accreditation Commission for Acupuncture and Oriental Medicine (ACAOM), 23

Acupressure, 19

Acupuncture
art of, 13–14, *21*
conditions treated by, 20
effectiveness of, 12–17, *15*
ineffectiveness of, 18–26, *24*
patient satisfaction with, *16*
procedures, 19
research on, 20–22, 24–26, 132, 140–141

Acupuncture points, 19

Acupuncturists, credentials for, 23–25

Adams, Mike, 12

ADHD. *See* Attention deficit hyperactivity disorder (ADHD)

AIDS, 46, 49–50

Allergies, 83, 84, 86

Allopathic (modern) medicine
acupuncture and, 14–15
alternative medicine and, 78–80, 119–129
drugs and, 28
homeopathy and, 29–34

Alternative medicine

attitudes toward, *127,* 128–129
can cure cancer, 67–76
can fight autism, 82–89
cannot cure cancer, 77–81
classification of, 115–117
definitions of, 52, 111–118
ineffectiveness of, for autism, 90–93
mainstream medicine and, 78–80, 119–129
medical schools should not teach, 154–158, *157*
overseas, 99–103
popularity of, 123
reasons for use of, *134*
research on, 131–136
skepticism about, 150–152
taught by medical schools, 145–153, *151*
use of, *116,* 117, 131
See also specific treatments

American Cancer Society, 73

American Medical Association (AMA)
cancer treatment and, 72
formation of, 31
homeopathy and, 33, 34

American Music Therapy Association (AMTA), 8

N

National Center for Complementary and Alternative Medicine (NCCAM)
  benefits provided by, 130–136
  on chiropractic, 51–57
  definition of CAM by, 113
  should be eliminated, 137–144
National Certification Commission for Acupuncture and Oriental Medicine (NCCAOM), 23
Nausea, acupuncture for, 13, 22
Neel, Joe, 104
New England Female College, 32
Nordoff, Paul, 8–9
Novella, Steven, 10
Nutritional deficiencies, 86
Nutritional supplements, 86

O

Office of Alternative Medicine (OAM), 139
Optic-nerve hypoplasia (ONH)
  about, 105–106
  Chinese stem cell treatments for, 96–103
  risks of Chinese stem cell treatments for, 104–109
Oxidative stress, 84, 85

P

Palmer, Daniel David, 53, 59
Palmer, J.J., 59
Park, Robert L., 7, 147–148
Patient-doctor relationships, 45–46
Pennsylvania School of Medicine, 146–150
Periwinkle, 78–79, *80*
Pharmaceutical companies
  cancer treatment and, 72–76
  drug promotion by, 28
  homeopathy and, 31
  paranoia about, 80–81
Pituitary gland, 106
Placebo effect, 40, 45, 123–124, 126
Placebos, *41*, 42–44
Positron emission tomography (PET), 9
Post-operative nausea and vomiting (PONV), 13, 22
Potentization, 33
Prayer, 117
Probiotics, 87
Publication bias, 43–44

Q

Qi energy, 33

R

Radiation, 71
Randi, James, 49
Randomized, controlled trials, 41–44, 123–125

Vinblastine, 78, *80*
Vincristine, 78–79, *80*
Vitamin supplements, 86, 92

W
Weil, Andrew, 152
Western medicine. *See*
   Allopathic (modern)
   medicine

Wheeler, Fred, 99
Wheeler, Thomas J., 151–152
Whittenberger, Gary, 58
Winterson, Jeanette, 39
World Health Organization
   (WHO), 36

Y
Yellow fever, 31

Picture Credits

© age fotostock/SuperStock, 66

AP Images, 140

© Art Media/Heritage/The Image Works, 30

© Bill Bachmann/Alamy, 11

© Blueberg/Alamy, 156

Radhika Chalasani/Getty Images, 94

© FB-Studio/Alamy, 114

© Tony Hobbs/Alamy, 74

© Dennis MacDonald/Alamy, 53

© Photofusion Picture Library/Alamy, 85

© Phototake Inc./Alamy, 21

© Felipe Rodriquez/Alamy, 80

Stephen Shugerman/Getty Images, 122

© Harry Sieplinga/Alamy, 149

© Stock Connection Blue/Alamy, 60

© Janine Wiedel Photolibrary/Alamy, 15, 110, 133

© Bill Wymar/Alamy, 41

Xinhua/Landov, 98, 106